LEARNING TO GO TO SCHOOL
IN JAPAN

This volume is sponsored by
the Center for Japanese Studies
University of California, Berkeley

Lois Peak is an employee of the
U.S. Department of Education; however,
this book was written in her private
capacity. No official support by the
U.S. Department of Education is
intended or should be inferred.

LEARNING TO GO
TO SCHOOL
IN JAPAN

THE TRANSITION FROM
HOME TO PRESCHOOL LIFE

LOIS PEAK

University of California Press

Berkeley · Los Angeles · London

The costs of publishing this book have been defrayed in part by an award from the Books on Japan Fund in respect of Carl Bielefeldt, *Dōgen's Manuals of Zen Meditation,* and Edward Fowler, *The Rhetoric of Confession: Shishōsetsu in Early Twentieth-Century Japanese Fiction,* published by the University of California Press. The Fund is financed by The Japan Foundation from donations contributed generously by Japanese companies.

University of California Press
Berkeley and Los Angeles, California

University of California Press, Ltd.
London, England

First Paperback Printing 1993

Library of Congress Cataloging-in-Publication Data

Peak, Lois.
    Learning to go to school in Japan : the transition from home to preschool life / Lois Peak.
        c. cm.
    Includes bibliographical references (p.) and index.
    ISBN 0-520-08387-3 (paperback)
    1. Education, Preschool—Japan. 2. Nursery schools—Japan. 3. Child rearing—Japan. 4. Home and schools—Japan. I. Title.
    LB1140.25.J3P43   1990
    372.21'0952—dc20   91-13628
                                                   CIP

Printed in the United States of America
9 8 7 6 5 4 3 2

For Mother and Dad

Contents

Tables and Figures

Preface

In 1983 I went to Japan to study contemporary childrearing. I was particularly interested in three- and four-year-olds—a period in Japanese children's life that presented a puzzling anomaly to Western students of child development. At that time it was the consensus of scholars that at home young Japanese children were indulged, highly dependent on their mothers, and unaccustomed to strict enforcement of rules for proper behavior (e.g. Lebra 1976; Vogel 1963; Norbeck and Norbeck 1956). However, in preschools and elementary schools the same children were consistently described as obedient, mature, self-reliant, and cooperative (e.g. Bedford 1979; Bingham 1978–79; Lewis 1984; Shigaki 1983). The obvious question was, How do Japanese children learn to make this transition?

This question was the subject of numerous discussions between Catherine Lewis, then a postdoctoral fellow at the Laboratory of Human Development at the Harvard Graduate School of Education, and myself, then a beginning doctoral student just returned to the United States after six years in Japan. She was the one who originally posed the question, and we used to discuss it for hours together. We speculated that the answer must lie in the Japanese home, in something that Japanese mothers "did" to their children at about the time they entered preschool.

I continued to wonder precisely what this magical childrearing technique might be that could smoothly transform indulged, loosely disciplined children into obedient, cooperative students. The best hypothesis at the time was that Japanese mothers provided their children with a strong dose of achievement motivation. A Japanese mother, the theory held, communicated to her children how important it was to her personally that they do well at school, and so the children tried to do their best away from home to remain in their mother's good graces (Taniuchi 1982).

In January 1983 I went to Japan to do eighteen months of intensive fieldwork in Japanese families and to observe the inculcation of achievement motivation in three- and four-year-olds. It quickly became clear that I was looking in the wrong place. My observations of families with children who were about to enter preschool netted few spontaneous remarks or replies to interview questions significant enough to account for the difference in children's behavior once they entered preschool.

Furthermore, both Japanese child development specialists and the mothers I studied told me in different ways that this new behavior was the result of the preschool experience, not prior preparation in the home. Although I was skeptical of the implication that the role of Japanese teachers in inculcating proper social behavior was more important than that of Japanese mothers, by April 1983 I had decided to listen to their advice. I arranged to observe the beginning of the year at Tokyo Preschool, a private preschool in a middle-class area of Tokyo.

I was amazed at what I saw. I had imagined that the children's transition to the preschool routine would be a relatively smooth one and that given the overwhelming influence of the home on children's habits and attitudes, there was little for the teachers to contribute to social training. Instead, I realized that the transition was difficult for many of the children and that the Japanese teachers were carefully and effectively training the children to exhibit the obedient, cooperative, self-reliant behavior they desired. I decided to reorient my method of collecting data to focus on the school's role in training children in appropriate social behavior.

Between April 1983 and the end of my fieldwork in July 1984, I divided my time almost equally between studying the first year of preschool and the first grade of elementary school. Only the data collected from the preschool portion of the study are reported in this book.

In June 1983 I began research in Mountain City, a fictional name for a regional city of four hundred thousand people located in Nagano Prefecture, in the mountains of central Honshu. There I chose as my primary field site Mountain City Preschool, a small private preschool located in the historic section of the city. I spent two weeks at the beginning of the school year observing classes full-time and about four more weeks doing so over the rest of the year.

Another six weeks were spent in interviewing Mountain City Preschool teachers and mothers.

To check the representativeness of Mountain City Preschool and Tokyo Preschool, I observed classes full-time for approximately two weeks at a preschool in a rural suburb of Mountain City. I also made observations for between two and five days in three other preschools in both Tokyo and Mountain City. Most of the data presented in this book are drawn from Mountain City Preschool, with examples from Tokyo and other preschools where appropriate.

I initially chose Tokyo and Mountain City as field sites on the assumption that childrearing patterns and preschool practices might be different in Tokyo than in a smaller city. Although some differences in philosophy, curriculum, and routines did exist in various schools, there was a remarkable degree of similarity between the two regions concerning the socialization of group behavior and the training in classroom discipline. Tobin (1989) and Hendry (1986a) also note that the preschools they observed sometimes differed in philosophy or curriculum but seemed largely similar in their actual practice of socializing children's behavior.

Every possible attempt was made to maximize the representativeness of the preschools and families studied while working within Japanese cultural norms, which require that the researcher be introduced at potential field sites through a mutual acquaintance. I declined introductions at schools that employed experimental or atypical teaching methods or were regarded as particularly famous or of high quality, in favor of schools that were considered unremarkable or average by the local parents.

On the advice of preschool experts in the Japanese National Institute of Educational Research, I selected preschools affiliated with Buddhist temples as the main field sites, for they were reported to be more typical in their teaching practices and less concerned with trendy and out-of-the-ordinary approaches to instruction. Hence Tokyo Preschool and Mountain City Preschool were both temple preschools. The other four preschools observed were either public or nonreligious private schools.

The influence of temple affiliation on the socialization practices of the preschools appeared to be minimal. All of the teachers employed by the Buddhist preschools had been trained at regular teachers' colleges and none of them reported regularly visiting a temple to worship. As I will describe in more detail later, no parents reported the Buddhist affiliation of the preschools as a major reason for choosing that preschool for their child.

Tokyo Preschool is a private preschool (*yōchien*) in a middle-class residential neighborhood in downtown Tokyo. In 1984 it enrolled 171 children in six classes—one class of 16 three-year-olds, two classes of four-year-olds with 34 students each, and three classes of five-year-olds with 29 students in each class. Tokyo Preschool was slightly larger than the 1984 national mean of 142 students in five classes per school.

The neighborhood surrounding Tokyo Preschool comprised modest condominiums, apartments, and older single-family homes. About one-third of the families had lived in that section of downtown Tokyo since before World War II. All children who attended the preschool were from local families and lived within walking distance. Most fathers worked as "salary men" in medium-sized companies or as local shopkeepers.

Mountain City Preschool, also a private preschool, was in 1984 considerably smaller than the average Japanese preschool, with a total enrollment of 60 children in three classes. There were 14 three-year-olds, 17 four-year-olds, and 29 five-year-olds. Because of the small enrollment the sex ratio at Mountain City Preschool was subject to considerable yearly fluctuation. Fourteen of the nineteen new students in 1984 were boys, although as recently as 1980 the entering class had been four-fifths female. Therefore it was not possible for me to speculate reliably in this study concerning sex differences in family and preschool socialization practices. Some caution should be used in generalizing the results of both the maternal interviews and Mountain City classroom observations to Japanese girls. In keeping with the largely male sample, the pronoun "he" will be used to refer to preschool children in general, whereas "she" will be used to refer to teachers, because virtually all Japanese preschool teachers are women.

The neighborhood surrounding Mountain City Preschool was in the process of transition from modest prewar-era single-family homes to office and commercial buildings. It bordered a small night district of bars, pachinko parlors, and taxi stands, and approximately one-third of the children in the preschool came from families who owned these establishments or worked in them. The other two-thirds of the children were fairly evenly divided between local families in which fathers had a high-school education and worked at local white-collar jobs, and families from other parts of Japan in which the fathers were university-educated bankers temporarily assigned to Mountain City. The banking families all lived in a large company housing complex not far from the preschool.

Although class background is not a popular variable in social analysis in contemporary Japan, there appeared to be some variation in childrearing behavior and attitudes between the families in the night district and the families of bankers. Tobin (1989) has also noted class-related differences in style and curriculum between Japanese preschools and Japanese day-care centers. Unfortunately, I recognized this possible influence of social class on family socialization only late in my investigation, and it was not possible, from the small sample of students in Mountain City preschool, to draw reliable conclusions. However, this issue is an important one for future research.

Because this study focused on children's transition from home to preschool life, classroom observations were most intensive during the first weeks of the school year, with periodic follow-ups. I also attended and recorded scheduled events for incoming and graduating students wherever possible. This included application interviews in two different schools, school visitation day in one school, opening ceremonies in two schools, and graduation ceremonies in two schools. In the other four schools principals and teachers were asked to describe these events in detail to check the representativeness of the two main schools studied.

I recorded data from classroom observations on cassette tape and in handwritten field notes. These observations focused on training in classroom routines and on incidents of misbehavior and student discipline. I then reviewed the tape recordings of teachers and students and transcribed disciplinary incidents from the cassette tape, synchronizing them with field notes recording physical behavior and nonverbal activity.

In addition to observing classroom behavior, at the end of each school day I interviewed teachers concerning their teaching and behavior management objectives for the day. Incidents of discipline or behavior correction were reviewed, and teachers were asked to explain what had occurred and why they had dealt with the situation as they did. This combination of observation and teacher explanation proved extremely revealing of how Japanese preschool teachers view the psychological dynamics of children's behavior and how they control it.

To better understand the child's transition from home to preschool, I conducted interviews of the mothers. Seventeen mothers whose three- or four-year-old children were newly enrolled in Mountain City Preschool were interviewed during the third month of the school year. The interviews were designed to determine the degree to which parental expectations and socialization were congruent with those of the preschool and the means by which each child had managed the transition to preschool life. Lasting from two to three hours each, the interviews took place in the woman's home and were scheduled while the child was at preschool. I conducted them in a friendly and open-ended fashion. All interviews were tape-recorded and later transcribed verbatim in the original Japanese. (See Peak [1987] for a fuller discussion of interview methods and a translation of the protocols used.)

Acknowledgments

My interest in Japanese childhood socialization began when I was an undergraduate in Japan, doing informal studies of Japanese families and various types of early educational settings. During this period Dr. Shigefumi Nagano, of the Japanese National Institute of Educational Research, patiently and skillfully guided my studies and encouraged me to apply to graduate school. Later, when I returned to Japan on a dissertation fellowship, his guidance, introductions, insights, and friendship were instrumental in the success of my fieldwork.

During my doctoral studies at the Harvard Graduate School of Education the teaching and guidance of Professor Robert LeVine and the influence of postdoctoral fellow Catherine Lewis helped me come to regard Japanese early education as a fascinating and thought-provoking contrast to prevailing American theories of child development. Indeed the central research question of this book grew out of many discussions with Catherine Lewis and the excellent example of her own research.

I greatly appreciate the kindness of the many people who helped me in various ways in conducting this research and in coming to know Japan. Most important are the Japanese teachers, mothers, and preschool children in Tokyo and Mountain City, whose warmth and generous sharing of their lives made this study possible, as well as my ex-husband and his Japanese family.

I also appreciate the assistance of other teachers over the years, particularly the members of my dissertation committee—Ezra Vogel, Jerome Kagan, and Catherine Snow. I owe a special debt of gratitude to Thomas Rohlen for encouraging me to publish this book.

Special thanks go to my friends and colleagues, Catherine Lewis, Merry White, and Robert August, for sharing their insights during hours of discussion about Japanese education.

Field research for this study was supported by a dissertation fellowship from the Japan Foundation and a Sinclair Kennedy Travelling Grant from Harvard University. Coding of some of the data reported herein was made possible by a Radcliffe Grant for Graduate Women. Time for writing and preparing this manuscript was made possible by a Spencer Fellowship from the National Academy of Education and a grant from the Joint Committee on Japanese Studies of the Social Science Research Council and the American Council of Learned Societies.

I offer this work to my spiritual teachers, in particular His Holiness the Sakya Trizin, His Eminence Luding Khen Rinpoche, His Eminence Dezhung Rinpoche, and the Venerable Lama Kalsang Gyaltsen. May this book in some way be of benefit to others.

Introduction

A new myth about Japan has entered contemporary American folklore. The harbinger of this new genre of tall tale of the East was a 1987 *Smithsonian Magazine* cover featuring an engaging picture of Japanese preschoolers captioned, "Japanese Kindergartners: Facing a Future of 'Exam Hell' with Mama's Help." Since that time other usually responsible popular media have followed suit with special reports on Japanese preschool education, characterizing it as obsessively examination-oriented, highly competitive, and Spartan in teaching style (e.g., *Reader's Digest*, July 1987; *Washington Post*, August 8, 1987).

Two excerpts give the flavor of these articles:

> Two-year-old Hiromasa Itoh doesn't know it yet, but he's preparing for one of the most important milestones of his life, the examination for entry into first grade. Already he has learned to march correctly around the classroom in time with the piano and follow the green tape stuck to the floor—ignoring the red, blue, and yellow tapes that lead in different directions. With the other 14 children in his class at a central Tokyo nursery school, he obeys the "cleaning-up music" and sings the good-bye song. His mother, observing through a one-way glass window, says that it's all in preparation for an entrance examination in two or three years, when Hiromasa will try for admission to one of Tokyo's prestigious private schools. (Simons 1987b, 44)

A front-page *Washington Post* article provocatively titled "Summer Camp Readies Japan's Kindergartners for 'Exam Hell'" (*Washington Post* 1987) painted a similar picture:

> Fidgeting at makeshift picnic tables in these wooded mountains, 160 five-year-olds, plastic spoons poised, stared hungrily at plates filled with curry and rice, cucumbers and salad. It was well past their usual lunch hour, but not one child made a move for the food that had been sitting in front of them for the last few minutes. Instead, they listened to a teacher extol the virtues of patience and forbear-

ance. "If you can endure like this you should be able to wait and listen to what the teacher says, to what your mother says, to what your father says. It is important to learn to wait and listen to what people tell you," the teacher intoned. . . . The underlying purpose of this three-day excursion was serious: these kindergartners were being prepared by professionals for their first encounter with Japan's legendary "examination hell." In a few months they will take an elementary school examination that many parents believe may determine the future of their children's entire lives.

The picture of Japanese early education in these reports neither accurately represents fact nor draws from the descriptions of Japanese preschools available in the scholarly press (Hendry 1986; Lewis 1984; Tobin, Wu, and Davidson 1987). Despite the inaccuracy of these reports, however, they apparently have gained credence in the popular media.

In fact, the vast majority of Japanese preschools are neither Spartan in atmosphere nor oriented toward examinations. They are cheerful, boisterous, play-centered environments even less academically oriented than American kindergartens. Such irresponsible descriptions encourage American readers to dismiss Japanese early education as a bleak and inhuman process. This is unfortunate, for there is much that American teachers and parents can learn from Japanese preschools. Because these and other myths and misconceptions about Japanese early education have begun to obscure American perceptions of Japanese preschools, the most pernicious misconceptions about Japanese early education must be refuted.

THREE MISCONCEPTIONS

Myth 1: Japanese Preschools Are Examination-Oriented

Although two-year-old Hiromasa Itoh, featured in the *Smithsonian Magazine* article, is reported to be already preparing hard for elementary-school entrance examinations, he is in that respect an atypical Japanese child. Less than 1 percent of Japanese children enter an elementary school that requires any kind of entrance examination (Monbushō 1985). Even allowing for the facts that the ratio of applications to admissions in some of the most selective schools may be as high as ten to one and that parents who desire such elite education for their children usually have their child apply to more than one school, probably less than 5 percent of all children sit for these entrance examinations.

On graduating from elementary school, 94 percent of all students automatically matriculate at local public junior high schools, again without sitting for an entrance examination. Very few Japanese children experience entrance examinations before the age of fifteen, when they enter high school. Only about one in five high-school graduates eventually enters a four-year college, and not all of these colleges have rigorous entrance examinations. Although entrance examinations are an important part of Japanese children's secondary-school experience, they are a significant factor in pre-primary education for only a tiny proportion of Japanese children.

Even among the 1 percent of Japanese children who do enter a selective elementary school, only a fraction of those children go to the type of examination preparation classes described in the *Smithsonian Magazine* and *Washington Post* articles (Peak 1991). On close inspection these classes are not as frightening as the articles make them sound. They are usually held only once or twice a week, for an hour or less, and most children attend them for only a few months prior to the entrance examination. The content of the lessons themselves is geared to providing experience with the testing format, helping children learn to focus their attention, and accustoming them to the types of questions likely to be asked by the schools of their choice. To an outside observer they appear no more challenging or stressful for a child of that age than a typical piano or swimming lesson.

The primary hardship involved in taking such lessons lies with the parents. Examination preparation lessons for preschool children are notoriously expensive. Most lesson programs charge at least ¥80,000 ($530 at ¥150 = $1) for the traditional enrollment fee and ¥5,000 ($33) a session, with one or two sessions a week. Only children of families who are able to make an investment of between $1,322 and $2,000 over a six-month period to improve their child's changes of entering a private school can afford to enroll. For this reason preschool-level examination preparation is beyond the budget of average families. Most children who attend such classes come from families that either are wealthy or have traditionally been members of the upper class, or both (Peak 1991).

Over the past thirty years in Japan, access to adult positions of prestige and authority has come to depend increasingly on success in the examination system. Therefore, for contemporary children to attain the social position to which their families have been accustomed, it is imperative that they do well academically. It is for these families, who strongly feel that they have a social position to maintain, that the rigors of the examination system hold the most anxiety. Generally speaking, the existence of examination preparation classes for a small number of preschool children in Japan is less an indicator of a nation of "education mothers" obsessed with status climbing than an anxious attempt at status maintenance among the elite.

We must endeavor to put entrance examinations in proper perspective in Japanese education. For most Japanese children, they are an issue to be personally contended with only at the juncture between junior high school and senior high school, not at the pre-elementary level.

Myth 2: Japanese Preschools Are Spartan in Discipline

Visiting news reporters tend to see Japanese preschools at their most formal. To greet the cameras, rows of uniformed children are lined up on the playground on their best behavior. The visitors are then treated to carefully planned exhibitions of "typical" classroom activities. The combination of uniforms, unison morning exercises, exhortatory speeches by the principal, and group classroom presentations leaves Americans with the impression that Japanese preschools resemble military establishments.

Although Japanese preschools train and value such formal behavior during some parts of the day, at most other times teachers encourage lively, boisterous, child-initiated play. Indeed, Americans who have spent long periods actually in the classroom (Lewis 1984; Tobin, Wu, and Davidson 1989; Hendry 1986; Peak 1987) remark on the extremely high noise levels, low profile of teacher authority, and extended periods of free play in Japanese preschools.

This continual alternation between strict formality and exuberant spontaneity is typical of Japanese schools in general and preschools in particular. Discerning the appropriate behavior to be exhibited at a given time and learning to switch quickly between the two modes is termed understanding *kejime,* or the ability to make distinctions. Accustoming children to full and enthusiastic participation in both the formal and the spontaneous parts of the day is an aspect of classroom discipline that receives considerable emphasis in Japanese schools at all levels. Understanding *kejime* is an important aspect of adult social behavior as well (Lebra 1976).

A second aspect of Japanese education that leads Americans to mistake it as Spartan is the frequent use of brief moral lectures and slogans. The homily on perseverance, reported in the *Washington Post* article, to which the hungry preschoolers were treated before their lunch at summer camp is typical of this type of encouragement. Although such exhortation to virtue unquestionably forms the backbone of character training in Japanese schools, far from being a grimly serious business, both teachers and students regard such ideals with balanced realism. Perseverance is to be admired and gently striven toward, but until such perfection is attained, teachers, parents, and students all display a relaxed and accepting attitude toward normal childlike behavior.

In fact, a well-rounded look at Japanese preschools sees childlike exuberance and spontaneity to be the natural mode of the day. Most teachers are cheerful and vivacious young women who show great patience and professionalism toward their charges. The classrooms and playgrounds ring with the sounds and lively motion of children at play. Indeed, preschools are one of the most engaging and spontaneous corners of Japanese society.

Myth 3: Japanese Home Training Makes Classroom Discipline Easy

Another common misconception about Japanese early education concerns the relationship between the home and school. Because Japanese classrooms are widely perceived as well-disciplined, many Americans assume that this behavior is the result of a similarly well-disciplined home environment. Japanese children, it is thought, are "naturally" more tractable and easier to manage in a classroom situation because their mothers require them to exhibit polite, self-reliant, and cooperative behavior at home.

In fact, this misconception is far from the truth. Many observers of Japanese culture have remarked on the indulgent and child-centered nature of the Japanese home (Vogel 1963; Lebra 1976; Doi 1973; Norbeck and Norbeck 1956). The home, Japanese believe, should be a place where one can freely demonstrate feelings of *amae,* or the desire to be indulged. This legitimate desire for indul-

gence encompasses the free display of feelings that in other settings would be termed selfishness, regressive dependence, irrita-
bility, and even petty tyranny. Within the context of the family,
however, and particularly when directed toward the mother, such
behavior is interpreted as a display of trust and intimacy. Japanese
mothers and teachers believe that this indulgence is necessary, particularly for small children, to ensure the trust and psychological
security necessary for good behavior in the outside world.

Whereas homes are indulgent, preschools require that children
learn they are no longer the center of attention and cooperate
smoothly as part of a group. The same child who at home enjoys
the patient indulgence of an attentive mother, who eats, sleeps,
and plays when he wishes and is largely unused to dressing and
toileting alone or picking up after himself, at preschool must suddenly perform these activities on a regular schedule, without assistance, in unison with thirty or more other children. Far from exer-
cising discipline similar to that of the schools, Japanese believe that
the home and the school are so dissimilar that it is difficult for the
family to teach the behavior the child will need in the classroom.

How do children accomplish this remarkable transition from dependent and demanding behavior at home to cooperative and self-
reliant behavior in preschool? If not through congruence between
home and school expectations, then how is classroom discipline
achieved? In this book I describe the process by which the indulged
Japanese child becomes a well-disciplined student. I focus primarily on discipline in Japanese preschools and homes and examine in detail the process of the child's transition from home to preschool life. Recounting this process of adjustment will also reveal
much about the role of the group in Japanese social life.

LEARNING TO GO TO SCHOOL IN JAPAN, OR HOW THE JAPANESE BECOME GROUP-ORIENTED

Learning to go to school in Japan is primarily defined as training in
group life. Rather than describing school as a learning situation, as
American teachers and parents are wont to do, Japanese refer to it
as *shūdan seikatsu*, or life in a group. The primary cultural goal of
the preschool experience is not that children acquire academic facts
or learning readiness skills but that they assimilate the behavior

and attitudes appropriate to life in public social situations. By seeing how Japanese teachers train novices in proper group activities, we also view the early stages of socialization in Japanese group behavior and attitudes.

Although it is widely agreed that the Japanese are a group-oriented people, the precise experiences by which Japanese children acquire this group orientation have not been adequately described. Contemporary anthropologists agree that cultural behavior and attitudes are a product of socialization rather than heredity or accident. Previous general explanations of Japanese group behavior have looked to the home and family for the origins of these traits. It was assumed that Japanese children learn the rules of social interaction in the outside world by practicing with their siblings and their mothers in the small society of the family and by observing how their parents interact with outsiders. Gradually, according to this view, the child elaborates and generalizes his experiences to the larger social world.

Although this process undoubtedly occurs to some extent, the Japanese themselves do not explain their own socialization process in this way. In the popular wisdom of Japanese mothers and teachers the home and the outside world are so different that the family cannot teach the fundamental rules of social interaction governing life in the outside world. The home is the home, and preschool is the outside world, and the two settings require different styles of behavior and habits of self-presentation.

This discrepancy between the public and the private has frequently been described by observers of Japanese society. It is institutionalized in the Japanese language and indigenous descriptions of the social world. The home, or *uchi*, is the private, intimate arena in which one can relax, let all of one's feelings show, and expect indulgence and sympathy from other members of the family. Within the *uchi* a healthy amount of self-indulgence, regressive behavior, and mild aggression are not only cheerfully tolerated but also encouraged as an indication of intimacy and trust. However, in the *soto*, or outside world, one must learn to assume a genial and cooperative public persona, in which individual feelings and desires must be subjugated to the harmony and activities of the group.

Uchi and *soto* differ for Japanese children just as they do for adults. There is a profoundly important distinction between the way children should feel and behave at home with mother and the way they should behave in preschool and elementary school. Because the two environments are so different, Japanese believe that it is the responsibility of the school to socialize children in group behavior. By observing the transition from home to preschool, we can watch the first lessons in group behavior for future members of Japanese society.

The everyday techniques by which children are socialized in group behavior are remarkably sophisticated and effective. Average Japanese parents' and teachers' understanding of children's behavior and their own responses to it are at once untutored and psychologically perceptive. This is true both of unconscious, culturally determined behavior and of adults' conscious explanations and responses to children's actions. Their common sense logic in these matters is not that of Western psychology, nor is it that described in the professional writings of Japanese academic psychologists. It constitutes an indigenous folk psychology, a rich alternative explanation of why children act as they do and how adults should react to them.

Pioneering Japanese psychologists such as Takeo Doi (1973) and Takie Lebra (1976) have described some of the key concepts of this Japanese ethnopsychology. But the sophistication and richness of this important area of Japanese culture is still largely unexplored. The results are of value not only to students of Japan but also to psychologists, educators, and those interested in the science of human behavior.

In learning something of Japanese folk psychology, we are forced to confront our own. Listening to Japanese mothers and teachers describing and dealing with children's everyday behavior, we realize that their perception of human motivation and behavior is not the same as our own. Even as "scientific" psychologists, we are forced to recognize the influence of Western folk psychology on our advice as specialists and on our own childrearing habits. Through describing how the Japanese socialize their children to become members of a group, I hope to encourage readers to reconsider how we accomplish the same process with our own children.

PART 1

FAMILY SOCIALIZATION OF SCHOOL-RELATED BEHAVIOR

1

The Different Worlds of Home
and School

SHŪDAN SEIKATSU:
THE MEANING OF LIFE IN A GROUP

Japanese parents and teachers do not perceive the family as carrying primary responsibility for training school-related social behavior. Teachers do not expect students to arrive at school with either a well-developed set of social and interpersonal skills or a good understanding of the limits of appropriate behavior. Similarly, mothers do not believe it to be their duty to manage the child's behavior at home according to rules similar to those the child will experience in the classroom. The two environments are naturally and properly discrete.

Japanese informants explain the reason for this difference in behavioral expectations simply: the school is *shūdan seikatsu*, whereas the home is not. *Shūdan* means group or collective, and *seikatsu* means daily life or living; hence the phrase means life in a group. By examining the implications of this apparently trivial, but to the Japanese fundamentally important, difference between the two environments, we begin to understand something of the deep structure of the behavior that Japanese cultural norms prescribe as appropriate to each setting.

As participants in *shūdan seikatsu*, children must learn that their own desires and goals are secondary to those of the group. A certain degree of *enryo*, or restraint in expressing one's feelings and modesty in presenting oneself, is appropriate (Lebra 1976). Children must develop a willingness to participate enthusiastically in group activities and must interact smoothly and harmoniously with others. Selfishness, or excessive assertion of independent desires and a determination to have things one's own way, is termed *wagamama* and, although an understandable aspect of human na-

11

ture, must not be allowed to influence individual behavior in a group setting. Individuals are expected to adopt these appropriate attitudes and behavior, almost as they would put on a uniform, for the duration of their active participation in the group. Once alone or at home again, the person can relax and let real feelings and preferences show.

The mother of a 3.10-year-old girl (i.e. age three years, ten months) described her daughter's adjustment to preschool *shūdan seikatsu:*

> I can see that at home she's more relaxed and vivacious; maybe you could even say she throws her weight around a little bit. Somehow I think that she's more open and free. When she goes to preschool, I can feel her *enryo* to the other children and the teacher. Even in her childlike way she keeps her wings pulled in more than she does at home. *(Could you give some concrete examples?)* For example, when she wants to use something at home she just uses it, but with her friends she says "May I borrow this?" or "May I do this?" I guess it's probably a rather unremarkable sort of thing. Because it's an interpersonal relationship [*taijin kankei*] you have to try to understand the other person's feelings and ask before doing things. You have to be sensitive. At home she'll say, "I'm going to do this" or "I want to eat this." Even if I say no, she'll still say, "I want to." Her natural childlike feelings come out. But if she's at preschool and she's told no, she'll just stop immediately. I guess that's what is called *enryo*. *(What do you think about that?)* I think that's all as it should be. As long as you have to relate to other people [*hito to kakawaru*] you can't think of only your own feelings. To get along with others, you have to act based on other peoples' feelings too. Yes, I think it's fine. *(Where do you think she learned how to show* enryo?) From participating in *shūdan seikatsu.* In a *shūdan* environment there is no other way that things can be. It's not something you can teach by saying, "Do this," with words. It's just something that comes from experiencing that environment.

Learning to keep one's wings pulled in and display proper *enryo* are the basis of the somewhat cautious and restrained self-presentation fundamental to *shūdan seikatsu.* Other informants agreed with this mother that these attitudes are learned in the group setting, not from parental instruction or family example. It is within the give and take of peer relationships in an environment that purposely lacks the understanding indulgence of the home that children learn they must make their *wagamama* (personal desires) secondary to the activities and harmony of the group. Japanese teachers and parents believe that this understanding is built through interaction with peers in the *shūdan* environment of the preschool.

By definition life within the family is not *shūdan seikatsu*, although from an American point of view the family might be described as a smaller group from which the child learns rules and roles to be applied later in the larger society. However, without exception Japanese teachers and mothers denied that it could be described as a small *shūdan*. In contrast to the English concept "group," the defining characteristic of a *shūdan* is not the number of members but the expectations governing their interpersonal behavior. In this sense the family is not a small *shūdan* because the expectations for interpersonal interaction are different. Within the family one can drop one's guard and express freely one's own feelings, however self-centered, and expect understanding and indulgence of personal desires. In fact, the right to expect such indulgence of *amae*, or dependency, is the primary characteristic of an intimate or private environment, and without it a Japanese family would not be considered worthy of the name.

Becoming a well-socialized member of the *shūdan* does not imply that a child's behavior in the family should undergo similar change. It is considered unremarkable that children and adults display self-reliance, cooperation, and perseverance at school and still remain dependent, assertive, and impatient at home. Such a personality is termed *uchibenkei*—literally, a home Benkei—after the famous samurai warrior Benkei. The appellation is considered mildly endearing rather than opprobrious.

Under the heading "inside face, outside face" (*uchi zura, soto zura*), a popular book on childrearing for Japanese mothers agrees that such behavior is the natural order of life:

> By the age of four, children's social skills have developed a lot and they are able to skillfully adjust their behavior to different social situations. It is not unusual that a child will pick up after himself at preschool, but not at home, or that at other people's houses he will share nicely, but throw a fit if he is not first at home.
>
> For both adults and children it is hard if one has to be on one's best behavior both at home and outside. If everyone understands and allows father to come home, relax, breath a sigh of relief, and act as petty tyrant and lord of the manor [*teishu kanpaku*], shouldn't we also allow children some room for difference between the way they act at home and outside? It is a cause for concern if a child is ex-

pected to be a good boy in the outside world and then comes home to a mother who is serious about discipline and is always keeping an eye on his behavior. Where can the child have a chance to relax?

European childrearing maintains the same strict standards both inside and outside the home. Children must always be aware of adults' moods to be sure they don't get in trouble. When they are not being supervised, children's behavior and attitude immediately change. With this approach, it is not possible to establish a warm and trusting human relationship. There are many good aspects of European childrearing which are worthy of study, but it must be said that this approach is old-fashioned.

Of course, this is not to advocate that there be no continuity whatsoever between discipline at home and in the outside world. The important point is that the value of the family to the child is not primarily as a place in which to be trained. Its most important role is as a place for relaxation and the cultivation of an abundance of love [*yutaka na aijo*]. It is necessary to have a family atmosphere that creates a child who thinks, "If mama were beside me, I wouldn't have these painful hardships [*konna tsurai koto ga nai no ni*]." Precisely because he thinks this, the child can do his best and persevere in the outside world." (Shinagawa 1982a, 46–47)

Indeed, the conspicuous display of *amae* in the home is an important method of affirming intimacy and trust and providing family members with the chance to indulge such desires and thus demonstrate love and affection. Learning to participate in the *shūdan* implies learning to switch between two codes of behavior—one appropriate to the family and one to the outside group.

The mother of a 3.4-year-old boy who had recently entered preschool noted:

I want him to be able to understand the difference between home and the outside world so if he becomes an *uchibenkei*, it can't be helped. It might even be said we sort of encourage him to be like that. It's proper that his behavior in the outside world be better. No one's a good boy in both places. If he's a good boy at home, I think he'll probably do bad things on the outside. So it's good if he acts *wagamama* [selfish, willful] toward me rather than doing it on the outside.

Perhaps the most extreme example of this difference between home and outside behavior was a 4.2-year-old girl who was so shy and self-effacing at preschool that she spent long periods standing quietly alone rather than participating in preschool activities. At home, however, she was so demanding and self-assertive that she completely monopolized a visit from the interviewer with a protracted screaming tantrum because she wanted to be included in the conversation. Her mother observed:

> The teacher says she hasn't really melted into the group of children yet and stands quietly along the side during playtime. If the teacher says, "Do this" or "Do that," she does things just right. She listens to the teacher and is nice and quiet, and the teacher has no complaints at all; she takes care of her own things and does everything she should for herself. But I can't believe it! It just can hardly be true. She's like this all the time at home [referring to the tantrum]. At home she always wants her own way. For a whole year she was home alone with me while her older sister went to preschool, so she got to do just what she liked. *(Why do you think she acts so differently at home and at preschool?)* Well, at one place or the other she has to really let herself out. When she goes to preschool, she holds herself carefully and so she really doesn't express herself. So when she comes home, she really lets herself out. You have to let yourself out someplace. The same is true for adults. At home she not only can't quit without giving tit for tat, she picks fights with her older sister all the time. She absolutely will not give in. She's completely different at preschool.

Neither mother nor teacher judged this extreme difference in the girl's behavior at home and at preschool as an indication of possible psychological disturbance or poor maternal discipline. Instead they viewed it as a temporary shyness and inability to gauge the degree to which she could relax in a group situation.

Indeed, the cultural assumption that the nature of human relationships is basically different at home and outside the family is reflected in the Japanese language. The words Mountain City mothers used to describe their children's relationships or interaction with outside people were distinct from words or terms referring to relationships within the family. *Taijin kankei* (interpersonal relationships) and *hito to kakawaru* (relating to other people) were used to refer almost exclusively to relationships with persons outside the family. The more simple and direct *ani to issho ni iru* (being together with Older Brother) typically denoted relationships with family members.

Even the word *hito* (people) is usually used to refer primarily to nonfamily members. This is an important distinction not usually drawn in reports of Japanese childrearing attitudes and behavior. For example, the injunction *hito ni meiwaku o kakenai* (don't cause trouble for other people) is frequently cited as one of the central goals of Japanese early socialization (e.g. Lebra 1976; White 1987). In fact, however, *hito* is not assumed to refer to family members. A mother's comment in one of the interviews reflects this attitude:

> (*What is the most important thing you try to teach your children?*) Not to cause trouble for other people [*hito ni meiwaku o kakenai*]. Not to do things which will cause people to dislike them [*hito ni kirawareru koto o shinai*]. Those things absolutely must be avoided. (*In saying "people"* [hito], *who do you mean?*) People outside the family, of course.

The legitimated causing of trouble for intimate others and the willingness to "let oneself out" to the point of exhibiting demanding and selfish behavior are the basis of *amae* and within the context of the Japanese family are interpreted as signs of trust and affection.

This discontinuity in behavioral expectations and styles of interpersonal interaction demarcates the Japanese worlds of *uchi* (home) and *soto* (outside) for adults as well as children (Vogel 1963; Lebra 1976). Shinagawa Takako, a psychologist who writes popular child-rearing books for mothers, describes the psychological difference in the two environments and the importance of experiencing both of them to develop a well-adjusted personality:

> In the warm, sheltered environment of one's own family, others do whatever the child says and focus their fond attention on him alone. If this is the only environment that the child experiences, he will lack psychological strength. Strength comes through the experience of insisting but being ignored, calling the teacher repeatedly but not having her glance in one's direction, and the personal realization, "I am not special, I am nothing more than one among a group, and if I don't act as everyone else does, I will be left behind." (Shinagawa 1982b, 59)

Neither style of personal interaction is better than the other in the abstract; in a healthy personality each should be exhibited in the appropriate situation. Japanese mothers desire to maintain a certain degree of *amae* in their child's behavior toward themselves and other family members while expecting that the child will learn to display *enryo* toward peers, neighbors, and others outside the family. For most Japanese children, the first time they encounter this expectation is on the first day of preschool.

2

Preparing the Child for Preschool

How much discrepancy is there between the behavior expected of children at home and at preschool? To what extent do Japanese mothers prepare their children for the transition to preschool? Interviews with the mothers of three- and four-year-old children in Mountain City Preschool suggested that mothers realize that once the child enters preschool, the expectations of *shūdan seikatsu* will dictate radically different behavior than family life has required at home. In addition to learning to inhibit egoistic self-assertion, children must become self-sufficient in personal routines for which many still rely heavily on their mothers. At preschool, children must use the toilet alone, change into and out of uniform twice a day, maintain rudimentary etiquette at the lunch table, and be responsible for organizing their own belongings. In addition to being expected to accomplish all of these activities with minimal adult assistance, children entering preschool are separated from their mothers, often for the first time in their life. The difference between the two environments could hardly be more extreme.

The official expectations of preschools for the degree of self-reliance children should have achieved before entering preschool are on the surface much higher than most children can actually attain. Mimeographed instructions given to parents several months before the beginning of preschool typically include checklists of requisite behaviors. They include such questions as "Can your child dress himself, including buttoning buttons?" and "Can he use the toilet unassisted?" Often these are even underlined to emphasize their importance.

Unofficially, however, expectations are considerably lower. During preschool registration interviews, mothers are usually asked whether their child can use the toilet alone. However, no schools refused to accept children who still required assistance. In fact, as we shall see, none of the three-year-olds and only about half of the newly entering four-year-olds at Mountain City Preschool were actually able to dress themselves and use the toilet completely unassisted.

Surprisingly, the mothers of children in Mountain City Preschool displayed a comparatively relaxed attitude toward preparing for this transition. Only three of the eighteen mothers interviewed had made a practical attempt to increase their child's self-sufficiency in toileting, dressing, or eating in the months before enrolling them in preschool. But in keeping with the cultural understanding that the two environments are radically different, almost all of the mothers indicated that they had worried about how their child would adapt to the new environment, particularly about whether the child could remain at the preschool without crying to go home, could perform self-sufficiency routines on his own, and could get along with the other children. The fact that little preparation had actually occurred indicates that to many mothers a strong emphasis on self-reliance and self-sufficiency is difficult within the context of the mother-child relationship.

How much difference is there between the home and preschool environments in the self-sufficiency skills expected of children? Interviews focused on two specific activities integral to the preschool day—changing shoes and clothing, and using the toilet. Mothers were asked to report their child's facility in performing these activities alone at the time they entered preschool and to what extent, if any, they had tried to train their children in these skills in anticipation of enrolling them in preschool. In the following sections I will describe the level of self-sufficiency preschool life necessitates and then indicate how well the eighteen children studied could actually perform these activities.

CHANGING SHOES

Children change their footwear numerous times during a normal day in a Japanese preschool. The cultural custom of removing one's shoes before entering a house includes changing from outdoor to indoor shoes when entering school buildings. Children wear indoor shoes (*uwabaki*) in the school building and on the raised open corridors between the classrooms. Indoor shoes are typically slip-on, rubber-soled, canvas shoes of a uniform color and design. The child's name is written with a felt pen across the top of the canvas. Indoor shoes are stored on a shoe shelf adjacent to the outside door in a space labeled with the child's name and identifying sticker.

Children arrive at the preschool in outdoor shoes (*dosoku*), which are used for traveling to and from the preschool as well as for playing in the school yard. Some more affluent preschools also require that these be of a certain style to match the child's traveling uniform. However, at Mountain City Preschool the child's everyday shoes were designated as outdoor shoes. Typically these were of the same slip-on canvas style as the regulation indoor shoes. Most children, however, had persuaded their parents to purchase everyday shoes with popular cartoon characters printed in bright colors on the canvas.

Using the toilet requires a third change of footwear. Children remove their indoor shoes and put on flat, scuff-type slippers (*surippa*) with the word TOILET printed in large English letters across the toes. These slippers are worn only in the toilet room and are left on the floor in a row across the doorway when not in use.

In almost all Japanese preschools children change back and forth between outdoor shoes, indoor shoes, and toilet slippers many times each day. Each time the child crosses the threshold into the schoolroom, shoes are changed, and the outdoor shoes must be replaced on the shoe shelf. When the child returns to the school yard, indoor shoes are removed and exchanged again for the outdoor ones. Only a few schools dispense with the wearing of indoor shoes in the school building. These are athletically inclined preschools that believe going barefoot stimulates the circulation in the feet and thus improves the children's resistance to colds and other communicable diseases. Some schools, termed naked preschools, go even further. During the warmer months the preschool uniform consists of only shorts, with both boys and girls playing naked from the waist up. In the winter a short-sleeved T-shirt is added to the uniform. Despite the lack of central heating in the classrooms, this practice is considered salubrious.

Japanese folk theories of health hold that developing resistance to the cold and stimulating the skin by contact with the natural elements develops resistance to disease and strength of character. Most Japanese teachers and parents, however, keep their children warmly clothed and consider the barefoot and naked preschools examples of harmless extremism. Yet even barefoot preschools maintain some elements of the Japanese custom of distinguishing among proper clothing and footwear for the school building, the playground, and the outside world.

Japanese families also leave their outdoor shoes at the threshold, but most preschool children are accustomed to going barefooted or wearing heavy socks inside the house. By the time they enter pre-school, leaving outdoor shoes at the threshold has become second nature; wearing indoor shoes, however, is new to most children. Mastering the distinction between the two pairs of shoes may take them several weeks.

Because Japanese custom requires so many changes of footwear, not being able to put one's shoes on and take them off without assistance presents a formidable obstacle to children's freedom of movement and participation in preschool life. Since the entire class moves frequently from the classroom to the schoolyard and back again, children who cannot accomplish this task by themselves must sit in the doorway struggling alone as the rest of their class-mates hurry by without them. Teachers turn an attentively deaf ear to the struggling children's pleas for assistance, calling "Yes, yes," "Just a minute," or "Start it yourself" while busying themselves elsewhere until the rest of the class is gone. Only when the frus-trated child is near tears or decides to go ahead barefoot will the teacher circle back and provide individual help and encourage-ment. Inevitably, the entire process is repeated only a few minutes later as the class relocates again or the child decides to play else-where.

Approximately half of the children in the class of three-year-olds at Mountain City Preschool still had serious difficulty getting their shoes on their feet when they started preschool. All seven of the four-year-olds, however, could accomplish this task with ease. For the purpose of this study, merely managing to slip the shoes on the feet was considered being able to put them on "easily." Difficulty distinguishing the left shoe from the right was not taken into ac-count. Most of the trouble stemmed from their inability to slide the foot forward while simultaneously stepping down into the shoe.

As with the other self-sufficiency skills, there was great dis-crepancy in performance depending on both the child's relative age within the cohort and the degree to which the mother had encouraged the child to perform this activity without assistance. However, interviews revealed that a combination of the child's willingness to do things for himself and maternal willingness to do things for the child played an important role in the degree of mastery attained. Here is an excerpt from an interview with the mother of a boy 3.1 years old when he began preschool:

> *(At the time Masato entered preschool, to what extent could he put on his shoes by himself?)* His shoes? Well, I guess I was helping him. When he entered anyway. And for a while he had a lot of trouble getting his indoor shoes on. As soon as he'd get to the shoe shelf at the preschool door in the morning, he'd start saying, "I can't put them on, I can't, I can't." I'd put them on for him then, because he couldn't manage the heel. *(Did he ever practice putting his shoes on by himself before he started preschool?)* Not at all. After he entered preschool was really the first time he'd had to do it alone.

The mother of a boy 3.8 years old when he entered preschool gave this response:

> From quite a long time ago he was able to put on his shoes pretty well by himself. Umm . . . I can't even remember when he became able to do it, it was so long ago. From the time he turned two he's always been very firm about doing things for himself. At first I'd try to help, but he'd say, "Don't, I want to do it by myself." So I would let him or he'd get mad at me.

In these examples both mothers justify their assistance or lack of it in terms of the child's wish to be helped in the task or to be allowed to do it alone rather than in terms of her own ideas about what the child should be able to do or of outside expectations. This pattern of explaining and justifying childrearing decisions and maternal behavior by reference to the child's feelings or wishes is a common thread throughout the interviews with both Tokyo and Mountain City mothers.

CHANGING CLOTHES

Changing clothes is an important part of the daily routine of Japanese preschools, as other researchers have already noted (Hendry 1986). In four of the five preschools observed in this study, children change into and out of two different uniforms each day. The quality and complexity of the uniforms varies in accordance with the affluence of the preschool and the families it enrolls. At a typical middle-class preschool the uniform consists of two sets of bags, hats, shoes, and smocks worn over the top of the child's regular clothes. The Mountain City Preschool uniform is of this type.

At Mountain City Preschool, the full main uniform, or *enpuku* (literally preschool clothes), is worn on formal occasions such as graduation or school performances, and an abbreviated version is worn daily when traveling to and from the preschool. The complete uniform consists of a beret, a brown button-down cotton smock with matching skirt or shorts, white hose, an identification tag, and a shoulder bag. For everyday wear, skirt or shorts and hose are omitted, and only the beret, smock, identification tag, and shoulder bag are worn. The identification tag is a plastic pink, yellow, or blue flower, the color indicating whether the child belongs to the three-, four-, or five-year-old class. It bears the child's name and is safety-pinned to the left side of the smock. This is the most basic part of the uniform, and even those preschools that do not have uniforms do require that children wear an identification tag.

The play uniform, or *asobigi* (literally play suit), consists of a different smock, a hat, and a pair of indoor shoes. It is worn over the child's personal clothing within the preschool buildings and the school yard. It is blue, with an elastic neckline, long sleeves gathered with elastic at the wrists, and no buttons. A large pocket in the front, embroidered according to the mother's fancy, holds a handkerchief and a packet of tissue. The play hat is of pink, yellow, or blue cotton, with the color indicating the child's grade level. Shaped like a jockey's cap, it is held in place by an elastic band under the chin. The hat is worn in the school yard and is removed when the child enters the classroom.

After arriving at school in the morning, children immediately change into their indoor shoes, enter the classroom, and remove their brown *enpuku* smock, shoulder bag, and beret. They hang them on a hook labeled with their name and put the blue *asobigi* on over their regular clothes. The child is now free to join in the early morning play period, although if he wishes to play out of doors, he must also put on the play hat and change into outdoor shoes. Whenever the child comes inside, the hat must be removed and shoes changed again. At the end of the day the play smock will be exchanged again for the main uniform, with its beret and shoulder bag, before the class is called together for dismissal.

In addition to these two uniforms, there are several other occasional changes of clothing during the preschool day. Many children are in the habit of completely removing their pants, tights, and underwear to have a bowel movement. Mothers are required to keep a complete change of underwear and outer clothing for their child at the school in case their clothes become muddied in the schoolyard or soiled by a toileting mistake. At Mountain City Preschool, during the summer months, the children change into swimming suits three times a week to play in a large, inflatable wading pool set up in the school yard. This activity necessitates four changes of clothing during the four-and-a-half-hour day—main uniform to play uniform, play uniform to swimming suit, swimming suit to play uniform, and play uniform to main uniform again before returning home.

At the beginning of the year, until children grow adept at changing clothes by themselves, teachers in all preschools reported that a large part of the day is consumed in changing from one set of clothing to another. During the initial week of school at Mountain City the change from main uniform to play uniform and back occupied almost forty-five minutes of the one-and-a-half-hour abbreviated school day. Furthermore, few concessions had been made in choosing the design and fastenings of the uniforms to make them as simple as possible for children to manage.

Rather than using smocks with velcro fastenings or pull-on smocks, most Japanese preschools prefer button-down styles. Although hats are no longer a fashionable article of clothing for Japanese adults, many Japanese preschools require repeated daily changes from caps for the playground to bare heads inside and formal hats when traveling. Getting the hat on with the elastic strap under the chin posed problems for many of the new students. During the first two weeks of school at both Mountain City Preschool and Tokyo Preschool, children frequently broke into tears over their inability to manage the clothing, particularly to turn the smock with its long sleeves and cuffs right side out again. Hendry (1986) also notes that changing uniforms was difficult for children at the beginning of the year in the preschools she observed.

Japanese teachers, however, appeared puzzled when they were asked why they place such a high priority on changing clothes as part of the curriculum. They explained that it was simply the way things were done in preschools and that the uniforms were required because they looked nice. They denied that the complicated uniforms had been instituted to provide practice in the skills involved in changing clothing. Rather, they reported that the children enjoyed wearing uniforms and that learning to wear them properly and to take them off and put them on was an important part of *shūdan seikatsu*.

Demarcating the difference between inside and outside or public and private settings by means of different clothing and language is a common Japanese custom. Not only schools but also businesses and organizations of all sizes require that their employees maintain two sets of clothing to be worn inside and outside the workplace. Being able to observe these and other distinctions is part of understanding *kejime* (social distinction) and hence is a vital aspect of traditional Japanese mores.

The strong emphasis placed on frequent changes of clothing is a central means of teaching the *kejime* appropriate to school life. The uniforms also serve as an efficient way of reinforcing collective identity (Tobin, Wu, and Davidson 1989; Hendry 1986; Lebra 1976). Teachers' patient willingness to spend almost half of the class time engaged in this activity during the first weeks of school demonstrates its significance as both a goal of early socialization and an unwritten part of the preschool curriculum.

How proficient were children in dressing themselves when they entered preschool? Interview questions focused on two of the most basic aspects of dressing oneself; putting on one's underpants and undershirt and fastening buttons. Responses from mothers of three-year-olds showed that four out of ten children had difficulty with buttons and six had trouble putting on their underwear alone. The six children in the four-year-old class were somewhat more proficient, but one child of the six still could not fasten his own buttons, and two could not put on their underwear unassisted.

These data suggest that it is not unusual for Japanese mothers to continue to dress and undress even four-year-old children. Although most Japanese mothers report that their children have mastered these basic skills by this age, in fact their definition of mastery continues to involve considerable maternal assistance to family members of all ages. Indeed, it is not uncommon for an adult man in Japan to expect that his underwear will be laid out and a suit and shirt selected for him each morning by his wife. This practice of laying out clothes as they are to be put on is reflected in the following answer of a mother whose child was 4.0 years of age at entrance to preschool and was judged by both mother and teacher to be proficient at dressing:

> *(At the time Yukio entered preschool, to what extent could he put on his underpants and undershirt by himself?)* I would lay them out for him in exactly the order they should be put on, and then he could do the rest by himself. *(How about the undershirt?)* I would lay it out with the front side down just the way it has to go over his head, so all he had to do was pick it up exactly that way and stick his head and arms in. *(How well could he manage buttons?)* By the time he started preschool, he could do them, although the top one on the uniform was hard because it's right under his chin. He could button his regular clothes, too, not just the preschool uniform. He seemed to enjoy buttons and usually did them rather quickly.

The mother of a 3.3-year-old boy who had considerable difficulty in changing clothes when he entered preschool responded:

> Well, when he entered preschool, he couldn't put on his shirt. Actually he could kind of stick his head and arms in, but he couldn't pull it down and get it on right. He'd get it all every which way and then he couldn't get any further. He really couldn't dress himself at all. And before he'd get all his clothes on and be ready, his eyes would light on some toy and he'd start playing and run off. He couldn't pull up his pants either and get them on right. I really had to do it for him. *(What about buttons?)* He could undo them but not button them up. It took a really long time for him to do even one. And he'd get sick of it right away and come to me saying, "Button me, button me," and he really wanted me to. He'd try for only a second, and then if he couldn't, he would start "Mommy, button me." *(What would you do then?)* I'd say, "Do it yourself." But no matter how much time passed, he'd still say, "I can't." And then he'd get disgusted and give up and say, "I won't. I'm not going to wear these dumb clothes." He'd get really irritated. So I'd have to do it for him.

The mother of a boy 3.1 when he entered preschool reported:

> Changing clothes was something he really couldn't do. I was really worried about it. They had to put on the brown main uniform and then change into the blue play uniform, but he couldn't undo the buttons and take his clothes on and off at all. After all, he's my only

child, and I'd been doing it for him, and he didn't have any expectation or habit that he should do it for himself. So when he entered, he couldn't change clothes at all.

TOILETING

In Japan children's entrance to preschool coincides with the final stages of toilet training. The preschool environment brings added complexity to as yet imperfectly established toileting routines. The comparatively high number of students in each class means that children must manage this activity largely on their own. In this section I will describe how toileting is carried out in Japanese preschools and to what extent children could accomplish these routines when they entered preschool.

Learning to use the toilet is made more complicated for Japanese children because two styles of toilet are commonly in use. The style termed Japanese is a porcelain fixture resembling a trough or hole in the floor with a six-to-eight-inch hood at the front. An adult faces the hood, straddles the hole, and squats almost to the floor, with buttocks resting near the ankles.

Small children use the toilet by being held over the opening by an adult. After completely removing the child's lower clothing, the mother supports the child's torso with one hand under an armpit and her arm across the child's back and the other hand behind the child's knees. The child is thus folded into an N shape with knees almost touching the chest and is held suspended above the toilet. Informants asserted that this custom of holding the child is necessary because adult-sized toilets are too wide for children to straddle safely. Stories of unsupported children occasionally falling into open cesspits when toilets were little more than two boards set across a deep hole in the ground suggest that the custom may have had its origin in safety considerations. Despite their apparently precarious suspension in midair, Japanese children were never observed to have difficulty in relaxing enough to release sphincter control.

Western-style chairlike toilets are common in newer Japanese homes and in more modern office buildings. But most homes, schools, and other public facilities are equipped with Japanese-style toilets. Mountain City Preschool was typical of most school buildings in that it provided scaled-down Japanese toilets that children could easily straddle as well as urinals for boys. The toilets were enclosed in six stalls in a single toilet room used by both boys and girls of all ages. However, one-third of the new three- and four-year-old children were accustomed to Western-style toilets in their homes and so had only limited experience with this Japanese style.

At preschool, children were expected to use the toilet whenever they felt the need and simply disappeared from classroom activities. During the beginning of the year teachers often reminded children to use the toilet before starting a new activity. One of the six preschools observed had a regularly scheduled toilet time, during which the entire class went to the toilet room; those who wished to used the facilities while the others waited for them. But during most of the year teachers left the timing of going to the toilet up to each child, with occasional individual and group reminders.

In the class of three-year-olds children frequently announced to the teacher that they wanted to *oshikko* (urinate) or *unchi* (defecate), and if the mother had warned the teacher that the child needed assistance, the teacher immediately dropped her current activity to accompany the child to the toilet room. Actual assistance with undressing, positioning, and wiping the child was rendered only after the child had made an effort to do things for himself.

The not-infrequent accidents and toileting mistakes were handled cheerfully and matter-of-factly, with an offhand remark such as "Next time you'll remember to go sooner, won't you?" Children who had accidents did not appear to be embarrassed and were never observed to be the object of teasing, even when they removed their soiled clothes and changed into clean ones in the middle of the classroom.

Mothers are much more involved than teachers in children's toileting routines. Caudill (1976) and Lock (1980) have commented that Japanese mothers derive considerable satisfaction from sharing and participating in their children's bodily management. Interviews with mothers of children in Mountain City Preschool revealed that as their children entered preschool, many mothers continued to be heavily involved in their child's toileting routines and that they did not feel a strong impetus to encourage their children to gain early self-sufficiency in this activity.

In Japan gradual development of toileting competence occurs in a somewhat different progression than it does in the West. From information gained in the interviews the following general stages can be deduced. (The process is similar for both boys and girls.)

During the first stage of toilet training the child is encouraged to signal when he wants to defecate or urinate. Even if he does so only imperfectly, the mother has long since learned to read his body signs. The child is disrobed and held over the toilet by the mother, who then wipes and dresses him again. Mountain City children whose families have Western-style toilets are still typically held over them as they would be held over a Japanese toilet. Although mothers' descriptions of this stage differ, they often call it "being able to use the toilet" or "taking off the diapers."

During the second stage the child still signals the mother, who accompanies him to the toilet and waits while he squats alone without support; then she wipes and dresses him again. Although this stage still requires the mother's presence and involves considerable assistance, it is termed "being able to use the toilet alone." In the third stage the child notifies the mother and alone goes into the toilet room, disrobes, and squats, calling for the mother to come to wipe him and put his clothing back on again. By the fourth stage the child still notifies the mother before going to the toilet, but manages to both take his clothing off and put it back on alone, and calls mother to wipe him only if he has had a bowel movement. In the fifth and final stage the child simply tells the mother *oshikko* or *unchi*. The mother then typically replies, "Go ahead by yourself," and the child manages the rest completely alone. Many Japanese children maintain this habit of notifying the mother into early elementary school.

The children in Mountain City Preschool were still accustomed to considerable assistance in toileting when they entered preschool. The mothers of all eleven three-year-olds and all five four-year-olds reported that their children always notified them before using the toilet. All of the three-year-olds and two of the four-year-olds still required their mother to wipe them after a bowel movement. Half of the three-year-olds needed their mother to attend them in the toilet and manage their clothing. Two of the three-year-olds were still accustomed to being held by their mothers over the toilet and were unused to sitting alone.

Within the context of the Japanese family, toileting is an important occasion during which children can demonstrate *amae* to their mothers. Rather than viewing continued assistance as an onerous task to be shifted to the child as quickly as possible, mothers' responses indicate an undercurrent of enjoyment in the mutuality this opportunity provides, as the interview responses demonstrate clearly. The answers of the mother of a boy 3.1 years of age when he entered preschool are typical:

> *(At the time Satoru entered preschool, how well could he use the toilet?)* He could use it alone. *(What about* unchi?*)* Well, I had to wipe him. Otherwise he did it pretty much by himself. *(Although he could do it alone, did he usually want you to come to the toilet room with him?)* Oh yes. Actually, even now, because he's sort of frightened or maybe lonely, he always says, "Come and stay with me." When I'm not busy, sometimes I think, "Oh no," and stay with him. When I'm busy, I get irritated *[laughs in mild embarrassment]* and say no. Really I shouldn't get irritated, but . . . At that time he could put on his clothes all by himself and even get them out of the drawer alone. And he could use the toilet pretty well all by himself, all except his pants. Even now, when he does *unchi*, he pushes his underpants and outer pants completely off, and they get all inside out. Then, although I really suspect he can get them back on himself, he always says, "I can't, I can't." Because I'm his parent, it's hard to know if he really can't or if it's *amae* that makes him say, "I can't." I feel sort of sympathetic and sorry for him because maybe he really can't, so then I sort of help him. But otherwise he can always put on all his clothes completely by himself.

In this passage two signals, in Japanese cultural code, show that the mother believes her son is demonstrating *amae* in his requests for assistance in the toilet room. First, the mother reports that she thinks, "Oh, no," but acquiesces. This common expression does not indicate that the mother is unhappy at the child's behavior but rather that she realizes that the child's request is based on a desire for *amae*. Although *amae* behavior is subtly encouraged, mothers typically complain as they acquiesce. This complaining signals to the child that the mother's acquiescence is a special favor because of her love and is not to be taken for granted.

The second signal that the mother knows the child is demonstrating *amae* is her comment "Because I'm his parent, it's hard to know if he really can't or if it's *amae* that makes him say, 'I can't,'" along with a description of her child's otherwise complete self-sufficiency in dressing. Certainly, the mother intellectually knows that her son is capable of dressing himself; but the issue is that in

her role as his mother, she should not apply objective standards of
self-sufficiency to his mildly regressive demands for indulgence. In
his toileting behavior her child is calling for her to allow him to
demonstrate *amae,* and her role is to allow him this indulgence.

An even clearer example of *amae* in toileting behavior came from
the mother of a boy 3.0 years of age when he entered preschool:

> Until shortly before he entered preschool, I had been holding him
> above the toilet like you do a small child. He became able to use the
> toilet alone barely two months before he entered preschool; he was
> just a little under three years old then. *(Although he could do it alone,
> did he ask you to come to the toilet room with him?)* Well, I'd sort of say,
> "Go ahead by yourself," but. . . . *[Laughs in mild embarrassment.]* It's
> just that, well, sometimes he'd get it pointed backward, and that kid
> just won't hold it when it's coming out. I still don't know what to do.
> What are other mothers doing, I wonder? If he'd hold it himself, the
> *oshikko* would come out in front with no problem, but he seems to
> think he shouldn't touch it. He never touches himself there. Because
> *oshikko* comes out of it, he seems to think it will get all over his hand.
> *(So you hold it for him?)* Well actually I've been teaching him to check
> to see if it's caught, and if it's pointing out all right in front, to kind of
> stick his tummy and hips out so the *oshikko* doesn't get on him when
> it comes out. But sometimes when he gets up from a nap or some-
> thing, it's pointing backward. Then it comes out behind and gets on
> his pants, and that bothers him. He's always worrying if it might be
> pointing backward. And if it's caught and not pointing forwards, I
> will tell him, "Fix it yourself," but he really has this feeling that it's
> not something for him to touch. So then I fix it for him. *[Laughs again.]*
> Actually, it's really kind of funny. I wonder what other mothers do?
> His dad really ought to show him how to do it, but he never has.

Although both mothers quoted here describe their children as
being able to use the toilet by themselves, it is clear that considerable assistance is being rendered. The initial reply that their child
can use the toilet "alone" or "by himself" is less an attempt to exag-
gerate the child's ability than an implicit taking for granted continued maternal involvement in toileting. In fact, this high degree
of maternal assistance is not uncommon. Here is an excerpt from
field notes I took during the first mothers' meeting of the class of
three-year-olds at Tokyo Preschool:

> Teacher opens the discussion of toileting at preschool with the ob-
> servation "When children eat or use the toilet, their family's customs
> become evident. For example, when children use the toilet at pre-
> school, some boys just stand in front of the urinal and wait for the

teacher to do everything for them, like their mother does." Teacher says that as an unmarried woman, she was nonplussed when she realized that some of the boys were waiting for her not only to take down their pants but to hold their private parts as well. She asks all the mothers of boys present to discuss how they teach their sons to use the toilet—whether they use the fly, take down their pants, or just lift up one leg of the shorts. Amid much laughter and embarrassed merriment a five-minute period of small group discussions ensues.

Within the Japanese context the staging of such a discussion constitutes an indirect request that mothers who have not previously done so should now provide at least minimal training in toileting habits. The teacher's stated reason for requesting increased self-sufficiency was not that children should be able to use the toilet alone at this age, or that rendering such assistance caused her more work, but that she was embarrassed to have to serve as a replacement in this privileged aspect of the mother-child bond. Teachers in Japanese preschools are generally unashamed about directly telling parents how to dress their children and prepare their lunch boxes and at what time to put them to bed; but the establishment of toileting habits is primarily the privilege of the mothers and is closely linked to indulgence of the child's desire for *amae*.

Neither in interviews nor in mother's meetings did individual mothers express a desire that their children rapidly gain self-sufficiency in toileting. One mother confessed that she expected there would come a time when she would feel nostalgia for her son's current lack of inhibition and his desire that she share these intimate aspects of his daily life. Frequently it is only the child's entrance into the less sympathetic preschool environment that provides the impetus for mothers to begin training the child in self-reliance. These themes are reflected in the following excerpt from an interview with the mother of a girl who was 3.7 years old when she entered preschool:

(Was there anything you were worried about concerning Midori when she entered preschool?) Well, you see, she wet the bed a lot. You could say she did it every day. Actually both every night and every day when she took a nap, even though it was only for an hour or two. I didn't know what to do because of it, and I didn't know how it would work out. I really worried. But she hardly ever does it now. It disappeared very suddenly. *(Why, do you think?)* When she entered preschool,

both her own feelings and her life became more disciplined. I think it's that. And also, when she was still at home, I think her *amae* to her parents was coming out in even just a thing like not bothering to go to the bathroom, so although she could do it if she would just push herself a little, she was feeling sort of slack or relaxed about it or something. You know what I mean—when she goes to preschool, nobody's going to help her or watch out for her. At least they won't do all sorts of things for her like her own parents will. So if she wets her pants, she'll just have to feel bad all by herself. Of course the teachers take care of her as they should, but things are more regular and disciplined. When she was still at home, her feeling was naturally sort of slack and undisciplined, so she was slack about going to the bathroom, too. She didn't sort of keep herself alert like she did when she first started going to preschool.

As these examples demonstrate, Japanese mothers realize that passivity about developing self-sufficiency and overtly regressive demands for assistance in toileting are an expression of children's feelings of *amae*. As such they are legitimate and not merely a stage to be quickly overcome. Because the nature of the mother-child bond is the indulgence of this *amae*, higher expectations or requirements for self-discipline most easily come from a less "sympathetic" and more objective source outside the family. It is this function that preschools and the exigencies of *shūdan seikatsu* serve.

3

Behavior Expectations in the Family and in the Preschool

THE PROPER ROLES OF HOME AND PRESCHOOL

Japanese childrearing experts concur with Mountain City mothers that the home and school have fundamentally different roles in socializing children's behavior. The home is a place where the child can relax and receive unqualified love. By contrast, the role of the preschool is to provide an environment in which children learn from their peers the unselfish and mature interpersonal behavior necessary in *shūdan seikatsu*. Experts and mothers agree that the home and the school share the responsibility of training children in the basic personal habits of daily life such as dressing and keeping clean. However, developing character traits and interpersonal skills such as obedience, cooperation, courtesy, and responsibility is usually described as the role of the preschool, not the home.

The following recommendations on the role of the family appear in *From the First Day of Preschool until the Last* (Okada, Shinagawa, and Moriue 1982), a popular advice book for mothers of preschool children:

The Role of the Family
One: Create an Atmosphere to Relax In

The family is the oasis of the heart. It is a place where one can draw a breath of relief from the outside world. It always has been and always will be the place where one can be the most comfortable.

Even after your child enters preschool, and in fact especially after he enters preschool, you must take special care to be sure that the family is a place to relax. No matter how much fun preschool is, unlike home, the child feels the pressure of being considerate and careful of his behavior. This shows that the child is becoming able to use different behaviors appropriate to different situations, which is a fundamental ability in the process of learning to become a member of society. If the family atmosphere is permissive [*kyoyōteki*], the child will have a feeling of stability from which will develop a calmly confident [*ōraka*] style of behavior. (59–60)

The next section warns parents about the importance of training their children properly (*shitsuke*). Interestingly, however, the type of *shitsuke* encouraged is training in what Americans would call personal routines or habits rather than personality traits or interpersonal interaction:

Two: Don't Forget to Train (Shitsuke) Your Child

At the same time the family has a responsibility in helping the child adapt to society. The child should develop good daily habits and self-reliance in matters of cleanliness, diet, elimination, clothing, and sleep. This must not be overlooked if the child is to be able to spend his days at preschool happily. For example, it may happen that dirty children are teased by their friends. A child who cannot put on his shoes even though he is in the last year of preschool may be rejected by the class group.

The child should develop good social habits such as saying "thank you" and "good morning," picking up after himself, and taking care of public property, in ways appropriate to his age level. These things are acquired naturally as the child watches his parents' example in daily life. (60–61)

The inculcation of what Americans usually call discipline or of character traits such as obedience, honesty, respect, and cooperation is conspicuously absent from this discussion of the family. It is described in detail later as the most important role of the preschool.

The authors justify their recommendation that mothers train children to be self-reliant in personal daily habits in terms of the child's adjustment to preschool rather than the child's own developmental abilities or family adjustment. Instead of arguing that self-reliance will create a happy family, in which the mother is freed from unnecessary demands for her assistance, they hold that it will make things smoother at preschool, where the child will then fit in better with his peers.

The tone of the warning is very mild. The examples chosen are perhaps deliberately unlikely to create a sense of urgency in the mother. Virtually all children are able to put on their shoes by themselves by the last year of preschool (five years of age). It is during the first year of preschool that problems typically arise. The authors' approach reflects the tacit cultural understanding that the nature of home life and the *amae* between mother and child make assistance with personal daily routines pleasurable enough for both mother and child that training in self-reliance need not be carried out too quickly or too rigorously.

Okada, Shinagawa, and Moriue open their discussion of the role of the preschool with a summary of the Ministry of Education's six official objectives for preschool and day-care centers. These are health and safety, social development, nature, language, music, and art. Then, apologizing to their audience of young mothers for the difficulty of this official material, they translate the official policies into the colloquial terms of Japanese folk culture:

One: Building a Healthy Body

The most important thing during the preschool years is to build a healthy body. Therefore, the preschool tries to have children become able to perform daily life habits by themselves, such as washing their hands, chewing their food well, being able to use the toilet without dirtying it, and removing a layer of clothing when they are hot.

This training is preferably the responsibility of each family rather than the preschool. However, at the preschool there are comparatively more opportunities to practice these activities than at home; so encountering these chances again and again, the child becomes able to manage these activities by himself. (55–56)

The rest of the section on health describes the importance of vigorous outdoor play at the preschool in developing a strong body and good health.

This passage reflects the Japanese folk belief that developing sensible, well-regulated personal habits is the foundation of physical and mental health (Lock 1980). Good daily habits are also an indication of good character and virtue. Both the preschool and the family must work together in training children in these fundamental habits of daily life.

Okada, Shinagawa, and Moriue assert that children have more opportunities to eat, use the toilet, and change clothes in the four hours a day they spend at preschool than in the twenty hours a day they spend at home. This improbable statement should be interpreted as suggesting not that children have more total opportunities to do these things at preschool but that they have more opportunities to do them *alone*. The authors tacitly assume that mothers continue to be heavily involved in helping their children with these activities at home.

AMAE IN THE FAMILY AND IN THE PRESCHOOL

Two primary means of demonstrating *amae* are regressive demands for assistance and egoistic expression of individual desires. Mothers' responses to the appropriateness of these types of behavior in different settings will help us understand their general attitudes toward the differences in behavioral expectations between home and preschool and some of the considerations they use in reacting to their child's behavior.

Mothers of the three- and four-year-olds in Mountain City Preschool were interviewed about how they would handle hypothetical situations in which their children displayed *amae* behavior at home and how they wanted the teacher to handle the behavior if it were displayed at preschool. Their responses were probed to get them to describe their gradually escalating pressure for compliance and the circumstances under which they would either abandon the issue or force the child to comply. Their answers reveal the degree of inappropriateness mothers attached to various types of egoistic and regressive *amae* behavior.

Regressive Dependency

Both mothers and teachers identified demanding assistance and attention in dressing, even when children are competent to do things for themselves, as a central example of *amae*. It is also one of the types of *amae* preschools take the greatest pains to discourage. Therefore, mothers were asked to imagine two situations:

> Suppose that your child is planning to play outside and says that he/she can't put on the shoes that he/she normally manages alone and wants you to help. What would you say?
>
> Suppose that at preschool he/she is planning to play in the school yard and says that he/she can't put on the outdoor shoes that he/she normally manages alone and wants the teacher to help. What should the teacher say?

Most of the mothers queried (ten of fourteen) indicated that after encouraging the child to put on his or her shoes alone, the mother would do it herself rather than bring the child to the point of tears. At preschool, however, most mothers (nine of fourteen) believed that the teacher should not help the child, even if the child cried.

The rationale behind the mothers' answers sheds light on the psychology of *amae* in everyday interactions. The responses also demonstrate the mothers' patience and their insight into their relationships with their children. The response of the mother of a 3.10-year-old girl is an excellent description of a typical scene of *amae*.

In addition, it represents the opinion of the majority of mothers, who indicated that they would eventually help their child put on his or her shoes.

> If she was just sort of whining, I'd tell her, "Put them on by your-self." But she has an obstinate streak about her, and you know how sometimes they just won't give up. When we have a battle of per-severance to see who holds out longer, I'll tell you honestly I often lose. I'm feeling, "It's something that you can do, so do it yourself," but when she gets really stubborn, I lose. I do my best not to let my-self do that, though. *(What about dressing and undressing?)* It depends. After all, sometimes they just want to show *amae*. Then I complain while I do it for them. She'll say, "Mommy, button me, button me," and keep it up until I do it for her. In that case I wait until I think that if I wait any more she'll start crying. Then I'll say, "Well, I guess it can't be helped. But next time do it for yourself, like you ought to." Actually, I'm watching her and taking into consideration if she's just whining for the moment but will actually do it in a little while. In that case I wait a little longer. But if she's not going to do it and will hold out to the end, then there's nothing else for it but to stick on a few complaints and do it for her.

This pattern of refusing assistance until the child's demands be-come highly emotional and then "sticking on a few complaints" and acquiescing is a paradigm of how Japanese mothers handle re-gressive *amae*. A mother's behavior in such a situation is not ex-plained or justified by reference to abstract ideals such as dis-couraging laziness or encouraging self-sufficiency. Instead, her minute-to-minute assessment of the child's feelings is the vital consideration. When a child is demonstrating *amae*, immediate acquiescence is inappropriate. In this miniature drama an emo-tionally charged tension develops because of the mother's repeated refusal and the child's calculation of the probability of her eventual acquiescence. It is precisely this element of uncertainty in the grati-fication of *amae* that both increases its psychological salience for the child and reaffirms the mother's power as she apparently gives in to the child's demands.

The mother of a 3.4-year-old boy observed:

> I suspect that I'm the one that usually gives in. Come to think of it, I finally help him. If he won't put his shoes on, even though I know he can, I help him, because I know that getting me to help him isn't really what he's after—he has some other unsatisfied desire.

Here we see *amae* described as a mode of direct communication be-tween a mother and her child concerning the child's deep-seated and inarticulated feelings. It is for this reason that *amae* is considered a crucial and legitimate means of intimate communication.

Of the twelve mothers interviewed, four said they would refuse to help their child put on his shoes under any circumstances. Two of these four immediately explained apologetically that they had only recently taken this hard-line stance because they had realized their child was extremely reluctant to dress himself at school as well. The responses of the other two might be classified as overly strict and unsympathetic by Japanese standards. The mother of a highly self-sufficient 4.5-year-old boy reported:

> I wouldn't help. I'd say, "I don't know anything about it. Take care of your own things by yourself." He'd probably whine a little, but I'd just let him cry. *(Does that happen sometimes about dressing?)* Yes. And if I know it's something he can really put on by himself, I deal with it like that.

The phrases "I don't know anything about it" (*shirimasen, yo*) and "Take care of your own things by yourself" (*jibun de jibun no koto o yarinasai*) seem brusque and unfeeling in Japanese. A mother's suggestion that her child's concerns are not automatically her own denies the bond between them and sounds particularly unsympathetic.

How do mothers prefer teachers to handle their children's *amae*-based requests for unnecessary assistance? Most of the mothers (nine of fourteen) said that the teacher should not help the child under any circumstances. In their reasoning, these mothers did not emphasize the importance of an abstract ideal such as respect for the teacher or the practical problem that many such requests might pose for a busy instructor responsible for a large group of children. Instead, they described the negative effect such a request would have on their child's relationship to classmates.

The mother of a 3.4-year-old boy commented:

> I wouldn't want the teacher to help him. What could a child be thinking to make a request like that [for help in putting on shoes] at preschool where he's one of many other classmates? Sometimes you just have to wonder at children's frame of mind. When he's at home, *amae* is a natural connection between mother and child. But at preschool, if the teacher knows it's *amae*, she shouldn't help him. A teacher is different from a parent. Even children understand that somehow in their own way. If children honestly can't do something, then they can ask the teacher for help. At home they'll show *amae* to

mother and come saying, "Button me," or "Come with me to the bathroom," or "Pull up my underwear," or "I wet my pants." But at preschool unless they really can't put on their shoes, they shouldn't go to the teacher.

Just why such a demonstration of *amae* endangers the child's relationship with classmates is elaborated by the mother of a 4.2-year-old girl:

> Although as her mother, I wouldn't mind if the teacher helped her, I wonder how the other children would feel, seeing the teacher let her do *amae* like that. They'd think that the teacher was especially nice just to her. And they'd feel a little jealous. I really worry what sort of reaction the other children would have.

Japanese mothers do not consider acquiescing to *amae*-based requests as encouraging laziness or lack of discipline. Instead, it indicates a special exclusivity and favoritism on the part of the teacher and a play for her love and consideration on the part of the child. However, because demonstrating *amae* so clearly points to the development of a close relationship, within certain limitations such demands may at times be legitimately encouraged. The minority of mothers (five of fourteen) who recommended that the teacher help their children with their shoes were clearly viewing the situation in this light:

> I think it's okay if children sometimes show some *amae* to their teachers. If he can say, "I can't put on my shoes," or something like that, it shows a certain amount of trust has developed between him and the teacher. You shouldn't just cut the child off, saying, "Don't be selfish [*wagamama*]," because it will hurt his feelings. But it's also true that if the teacher shows that attitude to one child, she'll have to show it to them all or risk being seen as having favorites. It must be a delicate problem for the teacher.

Wagamama (Selfishness)

Mothers were asked how they would react and how they thought the teacher should react to a hypothetical example of a different style of *amae* behavior called *wagamama*, or the selfish expression of egoistic desires:

> Suppose that one Sunday, father, mother, your child, and his brothers and sisters are all together and are about to have some watermelon for an afternoon snack. When the watermelon is cut, each

piece comes out a slightly different size, and there are large, medium, and small pieces. Your child says, "Give me the biggest one." What would you say?

Suppose that at preschool the whole class is about to have some watermelon as a snack. When the watermelon is cut, each piece comes out a slightly different size. Your child says, "Give me the biggest piece." What do you think the teacher should say?

The most mothers (six out of thirteen) reported that at home they would simply give the child the biggest piece:

I'd give it to him. It's really not a very important thing. He's still got first priority. His father and I don't particularly want big pieces. I'd just give it to him.

However, four of the thirteen mothers said they would deny the child's request because of the child's position within the family hierarchy:

Well, even without anything being said, I always give the biggest one to Father and so hold him up to the children. The children are satisfied with that. I always say, "I don't need one, you should give it to Father." Then after that it goes by size. The biggest child gets the biggest piece, and so on. Takatoshi's in the middle, so he gets the middle-sized one. They seem to be satisfied that that's the way things are. I say, "Older brother's five years old so he gets five pieces, and you're four so you get four pieces, and younger brother's two years old, but we'll give him three pieces anyway."

Some of these mothers would work within the prescribed hierarchy but modify it in deference to the child's wishes:

At our house, the biggest [piece] always goes to Father. But Katsuaki would still probably say, "I want the biggest one." But I'd say "Daddy's the most important person, and he goes out and works hard every day for you and Mama, so we want him to have the nicest one." Then Katsuaki might say, "Daddy's lucky, that's not fair." Then his father would probably cut a piece off of his own and give it to him.

At preschool, however, all mothers agreed that the child should not be allowed to have the biggest piece. Outside the family such a request is an example of inappropriately concealed *wagamama*. Although such feelings are natural and generally to be indulged within the family, they should not be expressed or gratified within the context of *shūdan seikatsu*. The mother of a 3.4-year-old boy replied:

I think it's natural that children want the biggest piece. So at home I'd say, "Here, I'll give it to you." But at preschool, because it's *shūdan seikatsu*, what you get in front of you is yours. If he complained or tried to get someone to trade him for a bigger piece, I'd want the teacher to tell him clearly, "You mustn't do that." At home you might say we let him show *amae*. But that won't do in a *shūdan* situation.

Achieving consistency in the child's behavior between home and school is not a goal of Mountain City mothers. Japanese believe it natural that a child be allowed to behave one way at home and another way at preschool. Although the interview included seven hypothetical situations, each set first at home and then at preschool, none of the fourteen mothers confronted with the full series appeared to be uncomfortable with the consistent discrepancy in how they recommended that behavior be dealt with in the two settings. Good behavior in the intimate, trusting circle of the family is not the same as good behavior at school. Learning to participate in *shūdan seikatsu* entails mastery of a whole new repertoire of skills, attitudes, and habits of self-presentation.

It is appropriate at this point to consider what insight we have gained concerning the question of how an "indulged" Japanese child becomes a "well-disciplined" student and to begin reformulating our understanding of the psychodynamics of Japanese childrearing. Is it fair to say that the Japanese child is indulged? The answer hinges on one's definition of indulgence. The connotations of the Western term do not fit the Japanese mother's understanding of *amae*. To an American, indulgence means overlooking commonly understood limits of behavior to gratify excessive desires or special requests. If it occurs frequently, it is believed to have negative effects on a child's social behavior. Japanese mothers' understanding of *amae* is somewhat different. Though *amae* also entails gratifying such desires and requests, within the Japanese family it is not an abrogation but a reaffirmation of commonly accepted rules of behavior. By showing *amae* to family members, a Japanese child is following culturally appropriate rules for demonstrating trust and affection within intimate relationships.

Furthermore, the Japanese believe that providing plenty of *amae* within the home has a positive rather than negative effect on social behavior. In their view, allowing children to freely express *amae*-based regressive and egoistic desires at home makes it easier for them to display the controlled social behavior necessary at school. Hence *amae* within the home is not indulgence but situationally appropriate preventive psychology.

However, if one takes as a standard the behavioral expectations of the Japanese preschool, it is not unfair to assert that within the home the Japanese child is indulged. The family's expectations of self-sufficiency and self-reliance are much lower than the preschool's. Family tolerance of *wagamama* is much higher and within certain limits is actively encouraged. For these reasons Japanese maternal indulgence raises fascinating questions about children's adjustment to the very different world of *shūdan seikatsu*. What is the nature of the new preschool environment to which the child must adapt? How is the transition from family life to *shūdan seikatsu* accomplished? In the following chapters we will consider possible answers.

PART 2

THE WORLD
OF THE JAPANESE PRESCHOOL

4

The Physical Setting of the Preschool

Understanding the physical setting of Japanese preschools provides a backdrop to the socialization that occurs there. In many ways their layout both reflects and encourages the socialization of students in culturally patterned habits of group life. Although each preschool is in some way unique in appearance and facilities, all share many common characteristics. Indeed, Hendry's description of preschools in southern Japan (1986) and Tobin, Wu, and Davidson's description of a day-care center in Kyoto (1989) apply equally well to the preschools observed in Tokyo and Mountain City.

The physical setting of Mountain City Preschool is typical of most Japanese preschools. The building is a single-story concrete and wooden structure situated in the corner of its lot, with a school yard on two sides. The school yard is a large open space of packed dirt and sand, with swings, slides, bars, and other climbing equipment around the edges. There is an area of deep sand in one corner, with a low, trough-shaped outdoor sink nearby. It doubles as a place for washing muddied feet and a convenient source of water for sand and water play. Another corner of the yard has a simple garden planted with various class projects, of which crocuses and long white radishes are favorites. Other schools may keep rabbits or birds in a low cage easily accessible to children.

After a heavy rain the center of the school yard in Mountain City becomes a four-to-six-inch-deep puddle, and the children enjoy wading about in their galoshes and probing in the mud with sticks. During the winter the puddle freezes solid, and children enjoy sliding as well as alternately chipping away at and watering the ice. Although Mountain City's play yard is wetter than most, many preschools encourage this type of vigorous, potentially dirty outdoor play.

Inside the building each of the classes occupies a separate room. Mountain City was typical of most Japanese preschools in that it enrolled three-, four-, and five-year-olds. Twenty-eight percent of Japanese preschools enroll only four- and five-year-olds, and 14 percent enroll only five-year-olds. The average preschool has about 135 students, divided into one class of three-year-olds, two classes of four-year-olds, and two classes of five-year-olds (Monbushō 1988). Classrooms for children of the same age are located next to one another.

Classrooms are rectangular in shape; they are small and functionally furnished by American standards. Figure 1 shows the arrangement of the classroom for three-year-olds at Mountain City Preschool, which was also typical of the other preschools I observed.

One wall is composed of full-length, sliding-glass windows that open onto the school yard. In front of the windows are a small desk for the teacher and a piano or electric organ. Along the opposite wall are rows of neatly stacked chairs and tables, which are set out and restacked each day to provide an open play space in the center of the classroom or table space for eating lunch or doing projects. On a third wall hang rows of double or triple coat hooks, each labeled with the child's name and identifying sticker, for outdoor clothes, second uniforms, and shoulder bags. The remaining wall has a small toy shelf, shelves for origami paper and other community art supplies, and a set of individually labeled shelves for each student's drawing books, crayons, clay, and other art materials.

Because most schools lack central heating, for four to six months of the year a large kerosene stove is kept in the room to provide warmth. A kettle of water sits on top of the stove to humidify the room, and a movable metal fence is set up around it to guard the hot sides of the stove. The fence also serves as a drying rack for snowy gloves, wet underwear, and various art projects; it is rarely bolted to the floor and serves more as a symbolic demarcation than a practical safety measure.

Despite an operating kerosene stove, most Japanese preschools are not warmly heated by American standards. During the colder months temperatures inside the classrooms are only 55–60° Fahrenheit, and the toilet rooms and hallways are unheated. Children wear several layers of clothing, including long underwear. Preschools with air conditioning in the summer are extremely rare.

The walls above the children's heads usually display class art projects. In virtually every preschool I visited, one wall was given

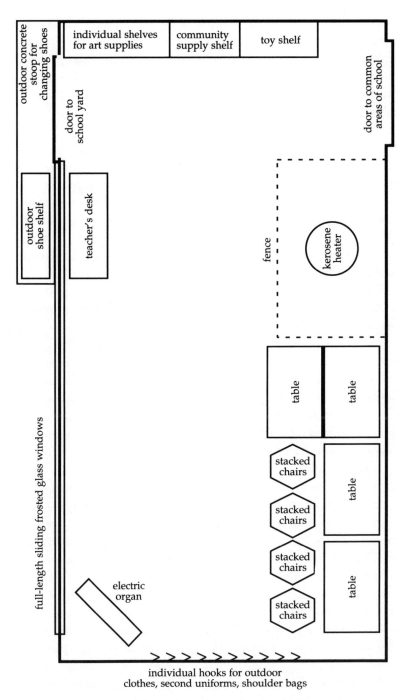

Figure 1.   Floor Plan of a Typical Preschool Classroom

over to a birthday display made by the teacher from construction paper. Such displays contain seasonal scenes of tulips, autumn leaves, or snowmen, on each of which are inscribed the names of children having their birthday that month. Despite the artwork taped to the walls, the overall appearance of the classroom is somewhat bare and functional.

Most classrooms do not have many toys. Hendry (1986) notes that the number of toys varies with the teaching philosophy of the school and that progressive and experimental preschools tend to provide more toys. Mountain City Preschool was typical of the more traditional teaching approach, in which the relative sparsity of toys is meant to encourage children to interact primarily with each other.

Those toys that are provided are suited to collective use and are multifunctional, such as blocks, colored paper, scarves, toy automobiles, dolls, and dishes. All toys are stored on one set of shelves and are not arranged into a "doll corner," "block area," and other predesigned activity centers.

The class shoe shelf is located outside the door that opens to the school yard. Here the children and teacher store their outdoor shoes when inside the classroom and their inside shoes when outdoors. A cement stoop, on which only indoor shoes or stockinged feet are permitted, separates the inside and outside areas. It serves to maintain a symbolic distinction between inside and outside and keeps the school free of sand from the playground.

A comparatively large proportion of the school's floor space is occupied by communal areas. These include a main entrance hall, a large assembly/play room, and a central toilet room utilized by both sexes and all age levels. The assembly/play room is two to three times the size of a regular classroom and is open to children at all times. During cold or rainy weather it is used for morning or afternoon assemblies. Because of its location in the center of all the classrooms, it is a favorite play area and is the primary site of interaction between children of different classes and ages.

Mountain City Preschool's playroom is typical of many. Along one wall are stacked huge wooden blocks for cooperative play, and gymnastic equipment, including a trampoline, vaulting horses, and mattresses. During free-play periods in cold weather, girls frequently play traditional line and circle games such as *hana ichi monme.* Sometimes a few children construct make-believe restaurants or freeway systems, which over several days or a week grow into sprawling constructions of huge blocks, scarves, and trucks or dishes. When this activity occurs, more and more children spontaneously become involved in the game, and the playroom may remain set up for several weeks until their excitement wanes.

Officially off-limits to the children is the teachers' room and its adjacent kitchen. Most of the floor space in the teachers' room is taken up by an island of two facing rows of desks pushed together with sides touching. Here the teachers gather to plan lessons, prepare materials, hold meetings, and enjoy each other's company.

During the regular school day the teachers' room functions as the director's office. Here she holds meetings with parents, answers telephone calls, balances account books, and nurses children's bumps and scratches. During free-play periods children wander in and out. After chatting pleasantly with the boys and girls for a minute, she mildly shoos them away. The atmosphere in the teachers' room is relaxed and friendly, and visitors at any time are welcomed with a folding chair by the kerosene stove, a hot cup of tea, and a plate of cookies.

5

The Roles of Teachers, Parents, and Students

PRINCIPALS AND DIRECTORS

The main participants in the daily life of a Japanese preschool are the director, the teachers, the children, and the mothers. Officially, however, the principal (*enchō sensei*) is in charge of the school. In fact, most principals are physically present at their preschools only part-time or irregularly and have little more than a cursory acquaintance with the children and the daily life of the school. They have usually been appointed to their position on retirement from another job within the field of education. Their average age is sixty-three years old (Monbushō 1986b, 282). The principal functions more as an honorary adviser than a day-to-day manager. Almost 40 percent of principals have other occupational responsibilities outside the preschool. Only 1 percent have any teaching responsibilities (Monbushō 1986b, 26).

When principals do visit their preschool, their primary role is to officiate at public functions and serve as a financial adviser and liaison between the preschool and its supporting organization. According to Ministry of Education statistics, 91 percent of Japanese preschool principals are men (Monbushō 1986b, 282), in sharp contrast with the teachers, virtually all of whom are women.

The day-to-day management of the school and its affairs is usually delegated to a full-time director (*kyotō sensei* or *shuji sensei*). Typically, the director is a woman, with twenty to thirty years more teaching experience than the regular teachers, who has spent her entire career at that particular school. Only 5 percent of preschool directors have teaching responsibilities (Monbushō 1986b, 27). Directors serve as an invaluable resource to principals, teachers, and parents because of their intimate knowledge of school policy and tradition and their wealth of experience with children and problems of all kinds.

The Ministry of Education reports that 86 percent of preschool directors are women and that their average age is 51 years (Monbushō 1986b, 282). According to ministry statistics, only about one preschool in three has an officially appointed director. Although virtually all preschools have a senior teacher who functions as the main administrator and adviser to the other teachers, preschools are not officially required to fill this position to qualify for authorization (Monbushō 1981). The fact that comparatively few preschools report the presence of an official director may reflect both the various terms in use to describe the position and the fact that senior teachers may be acting in this capacity without official appointment.

In both Mountain City Preschool and Tokyo Preschool the principal and director matched this statistical norm. The directors were veteran women teachers, forty to fifty years of age, who managed the preschool quietly, confidently, and efficiently. In each case the principal was an older man, past sixty years of age, whose declining physical condition and myriad responsibilities made him an infrequent but honored guest at the preschool. In many ways the roles of the principal and director of a Japanese preschool parallel those of parents in a stereotypical Japanese home. The principal is the respected but chronically absent father, the director the wise, capable, and efficient mother.

TEACHERS

Preschool teachers (*sensei*) are usually young women in their twenties. Ministry of Education statistics show that in 1986, 99.6 percent of preschool teachers were women (Monbushō 1986b, 282). The average age was twenty-seven years and almost half were under the age of twenty-five.

Preschool teaching in Japan is a relatively prestigious job for young women. The salary is comparable to that received by college educated women elsewhere in the economy (Tobin, Wu, and Davidson 1989). It is the third most popular course of study at the junior-college level, after literature and home economics (Statistics Bureau 1988, 658). It attracts energetic, confident, middle-class and upper middle-class young women who typically devote themselves to teaching until they retire from outside employment when their first child is born (Monbushō 1987, 436). With rare exceptions, they are well educated, cheerful, and self-possessed in their approach to children.

Japanese preschool teachers have an above-average education and must pass a certification exam to be qualified as a teacher. Although only about one in three Japanese high-school graduates enters a two- or four-year college (United States Department of Education 1987, 78), 85 percent of preschool teachers have a junior-college diploma. These teachers have all majored in preschool and early education and have passed a prefectural certification examination. Their junior-college training includes a minimum of eighteen credits in general education, eight in teaching subjects, and eighteen in professional subjects (Monbushō 1981). It also requires piano training so that teachers are able to play well enough to accompany their classes in singing songs. Ninety percent of Japanese preschools do not employ any uncertified teachers (Monbushō 1986b, 27). Boocock (1989) notes:

> [These high] professional qualifications and affiliations do not, however, satisfactorily explain the impressive performance in the classroom by these young, mainly female professionals. Foreign visitors to Japanese preschools routinely report . . . on the teachers' skills in "managing" young children, often in groups that are exceptionally large by Western standards. Indeed, the wisdom and tolerance displayed by preschool teachers and *hobo-san* [day-care teachers] often belies their youth and rather brief professional experience. (56–57).

Japanese preschool teachers work an eight- or nine-hour day, arriving at school at about 8:00 A.M. and leaving for home between 4:00 and 5:00 P.M. In most cases there is only one teacher for each classroom. Legally forty children may be assigned to a single class (Kodama 1983), although the national average is about twenty-eight children per class (Monbushō 1986b, 26). Only about 10 percent of preschools employ a teaching assistant or specialist in a particular subject (Monbushō 1986b, 28), who may help out as necessary in the classroom or teach special activities such as art. Occasionally the director may lend a hand in younger classes during the difficult first weeks of the year or when special activities require extra help for the regular teacher.

In interactions with each other Japanese teachers are remarkably positive, supportive, and industrious. After the children have left for the day, the atmosphere in the teachers' room is one of girlish high spirits and sisterly companionship. Teachers remain at the preschool until late afternoon, cleaning and sweeping the school, discussing and jointly planning activities, preparing teaching materials, drinking tea, and generally enjoying each other's company.

Despite the friendliness of the teachers' relationships with each other, however, there is a subtle hierarchy within the group. Each teacher defers to her colleagues with one or two years more teaching experience, who in turn give advice and assistance to the younger ones. All regular teachers defer to the director in a manner that carefully calibrates spontaneity and reserve. But when the principal is present in the teachers' room, they remain politely silent, not speaking unless spoken to, holding their normal buoyancy respectfully in check.

STUDENTS

Articles in both the Japanese and American popular press suggest that Japanese children are enrolled in preschools by ambitious mothers hoping that preschool will help their children enter a prestigious elementary school and eventually an elite university. For most Japanese mothers, however, a preschool's academic standing is not an important criterion for selection. Tobin, Wu, and Davidson (1989) estimate that academically oriented and examination-conscious preschools represent only 5 percent of the preschools in Japan. A questionnaire study of the pre-elementary educational experience of children from a variety of social backgrounds found that special preparation during the preschool years is largely limited to upper-class families who can afford the high tuitions (Peak 1991).

In Mountain City Preschool and Tokyo Preschool, as in most Japanese preschools, almost all students live within walking distance or within a ten-to-fifteen-minute commute on the back of the mother's bicycle. Interviews with mothers and the reports of principals at Tokyo and other preschools suggest that most Japanese mothers send their children to preschool with the expectation that they will make friends and learn to participate in life in a group. They try to choose a preschool close to home so that their children will be able to maintain and enlarge their network of friendships with other neighborhood children. Each mother usually tries to send all of her children to the same preschool, establishing a long-term connection between the preschool and the family.

These findings about Japanese mothers' priorities in choosing a preschool were echoed in *By the Time Your Child Is Three* (*San sai made ni kore dake wa*), a book of childrearing advice by Shinagawa Takako (1982b), a well-known psychologist. These are her recommendations, in slightly abbreviated form:

Choosing a Preschool

Look for the following attributes in choosing your child's preschool:

1. The school should be within walking distance from home. Children learn a lot about daily life and society by walking to school.

2. Choose a school that your child's friends in the neighborhood also attend. This will be fun for your child and give him confidence.

3. The childrearing approach of the preschool should fit that of your family. Does the preschool have a carefree [*nobi-nobi*] or disciplined philosophy?

4. Watch out for preschools with a reputation for examination preparation or stuffing [*tsumikomu*] children with knowledge. Be cautious of preschools that advertise piano, ballet, or English conversation lessons. These have forgotten the real essence of preschool education. Avoid preschools that boast of placing graduates in famous elementary schools.

5. Both the principal and the teachers should have an interest in trying new things and expanding their knowledge [*kenkyū iyoku*].

6. The principal, teachers, and board of directors should work together harmoniously.

7. Talk with mothers whose children are currently enrolled in the preschool.

8. Consider your own preferences, outlook on life, and family situation in your decision. (220–221)

The reasons that mothers reported for choosing Mountain City Preschool reflect such precepts as these, although only one of the mothers reported reading any childrearing advice books during the past year, and none had read Shinagawa's book. Table 1 shows the reasons they cited.

The following response by the mother of a four-year-old boy was typical in both the reasons she gives and the way she made her decision:

(*I'm sure that before you chose Mountain City Preschool, you must have considered other places that Noboyuki could have gone to. How is it that you came to send him to Mountain City Preschool?*) Well, there are two day-

Table 1   Reasons Cited by Mothers of Three- and Four-Year-Olds
for Choosing Mountain City Preschool, 1984 (n = 18)

Reason	Number of Mothers
Proximity to home	9
Family did not qualify for day-care center	7
Siblings attend or parents attended	6
Children are allowed to play freely	6
Neighbor's children attend	4
Teachers' friendliness and accessibility	3
Social connections with preschool administrators	2
Other	3
Total	40

care centers in this area. But to get into them, it seems you have to meet the criteria. The people who meet the criteria are enrolled first. Because I don't work, they'd say I'm able to look after Noboyuki myself and that I don't need a day-care center, so I'd be turned down. So that leaves preschools. There's one a ways from here, and then Mountain City Preschool, which is the closest. Just a couple of doors away there's a lady who sends her child to Mountain City Preschool. I asked her about it and she said that they let the kids play very freely, they can get muddy if they want, and it's a great place. She said that if you agree with that approach, why don't you send Noboyuki? My husband and I liked that, and it was near the house, so I decided to send him there. *(Were there any other reasons?)* Not particularly. *(About the fact that it's a Buddhist preschool . . .)* I didn't particularly mind. It didn't make any difference one way or the other.

Interestingly, about one-third of the mothers suggested that they would have seriously considered a day-care center if their children had been eligible for one. No mothers spontaneously mentioned a desire to enroll their child in a Buddhist preschool as a reason for choosing Mountain City Preschool. When specifically asked, only one mother expressed any feelings about it. She said that she had initially considered it a drawback yet decided to enroll her child anyway because the preschool was located so close to their home.

Preschools follow the procedure used in elementary schools for assigning children to classes. The child's age on April 1 is the determining factor. No exceptions to this policy are made for early or late bloomers, at either the elementary-school or preschool level.

Because the first day of school falls variously during the first or second week of April, it is not uncommon that the oldest child in the three-year-old class has already turned four. Particularly in preschool and early elementary school grades, both mothers and teachers are aware of the resultant age-related differences in physical and social maturity and commonly explain children's behavior as being related to their early or late birthday.

At the time of registration children are assigned by age to a class of three-year-olds, four-year-olds, or five-year-olds. About 12 percent of all preschools have at least one class mixing children of different ages (Monbushō, 1986b), usually because there is a shortage of either students or instructors. Each age group is designated by a color, which serves as a name for the entire age group; it is also the color of their caps and badges. This color coding is standardized in all the schools observed; pink for three-year-olds, yellow for four-year-olds, and blue for five-year-olds. In addition, each classroom group is referred to by a name, usually that of a flower, such as rose, lily, or dandelion. All children wear name tags on their uniforms, which by their color and shape identify the child by classroom and age group. Thus a child is simultaneously a member of two classes. In various situations he may be referred to as a pink class member (three-year-olds) or a dandelion class member (his particular classroom group).

Class size depends on the enrollment of the school and the number of children in a given neighborhood. Although a class may range from ten to forty children, the national average is twenty-eight (Monbushō 1986b, 26). Japanese teachers believe that large classes are better than small ones because they encourage peer relationships and interaction. They also lower the salience of the teacher as the focus of the students' attention (Tobin, Wu, and Davidson, 1987, 10).

Tobin, Wu, and Davidson found that Japanese teachers' comfort with larger classes is related to their beliefs about the difference between the roles of teachers and mothers. Preschool teachers believe that they should not establish dyadic motherlike relationships with each of the children. Rather, the teacher's job is to facilitate and encourage the establishment of peer relationships and group interaction. Large class size makes it more difficult for children to engage the teacher on a one-to-one basis.

Mountain City Preschool enrolled 14 three-year-olds, 17 four-year-olds, and 29 five-year-olds. These small classes were a source of serious concern to the teachers and principal. This concern was not financial; the Buddhist temple contributed a substantial portion of the operating expenses. But the teachers felt the small class size had a negative impact on the students' social environment. They believed that larger classes would have provided a broader range of personalities for children to experience and would have generated more enthusiasm and shared excitement in group activities.

Partly as an outgrowth of the desire to provide a diverse social environment, and partly owing to a scarcity of special preschools for handicapped children, it is common for children with light to moderate disabilities to be enrolled in regular preschools. All but one of the five preschools I observed contained one or two children who would later be unable to attend regular elementary schools. Mountain City Preschool had one completely deaf child in the class of four-year-olds and one child with Down's syndrome in the class of five-year-olds. These children were treated the same as other students, except for receiving a few moments of extra assistance from the teacher or classmates. Teachers seemed to regard these children as a special professional challenge and were never heard to complain about the added responsibilities they entailed. The handicapped children copied closely the activities of their classmates and were remarkably well integrated into the class. When necessary, other children were assigned to lead them by the hand and assure their participation in the group.

MOTHERS

Mothers in Japanese preschools play an extremely important and time-consuming supporting role. However, in contrast to American preschools, some of which are parent cooperatives, Japanese mothers never work in the classroom as instructional aides or assistant teachers. In fact, mothers avoid entering the classroom while class is in session except on carefully planned observation days for parents.

Teachers explain that the presence of mothers in the classroom inhibits the development of children's friendships and peer interaction. They assert that even during short maternal visits children tend to show *amae* to their mothers, not to join in activities with their peers, and to be less willing to do things for themselves. It is as though the behavior appropriate to mother-child interaction and that appropriate to group life in the classroom are so different that the coincidence of the two sets of expectations is believed to be confusing for the child.

Although not present in the classroom, mothers are expected to be active in preschool-related activities. All are expected to participate in monthly parent-teacher association (PTA) meetings and various rotating work groups. Each mother also belongs to a PTA-sponsored mothers' club, which meets once or twice a month during school hours for group singing, hiking, or needlecraft.

A smaller group of mothers assumes considerable administrative responsibility through the PTA. Each class (as well as each neighborhood) chooses two representatives to the PTA. In addition, four regular PTA officers are chosen from the school at large. In a given year at Mountain City Preschool, approximately one mother in five holds a PTA office, and these positions are rotated each year.

Holding office is not a duty that is sought after as it entails much extra work and responsibility. At the meetings in which the PTA representatives are selected, typically each mother in turn offers some excuse as to why it is impossible for her to take on the position. Those with the least plausible excuse for declining are then good-humoredly pressured into accepting. These are usually mothers with some experience at the preschool and no younger children still at home.

For the mothers of preschool children, preschool-related activities and acquaintances form a new social network beyond immediate neighbors and extended family. For the first time in a woman's life, the network is defined in terms of her child's activities and interests rather than her own. This is the beginning of a pattern that will continue throughout her child's school career.

Secretaries and other support staff for the preschool are rendered unnecessary by a combination of maternal assistance with administrative matters and the late-afternoon activities of the regular teachers. Mothers assist in collecting tuition and other fees, producing periodic newsletters, organizing special gardening and cleaning projects, staging festivals and excursions, and cooking the twice-weekly hot lunch. More important than the staff salaries saved is the belief that it is the responsibility of the students and their parents to demonstrate respect for the teachers and activities of the preschool by doing the support work necessary to create a good learning environment.

In addition to organized group activities, mothers of children enrolled in Japanese preschools must devote time to assisting their child in various ways each school day. All preschools required each mother personally to bring her child to the preschool gate or to the school bus stop each morning and return for him in the afternoon. Consistent tardiness at dismissal time or "bike-pooling" with other mothers from the neighborhood was held in extreme disfavor by the teachers. Such behavior was discussed among the teachers as worrisome evidence of the mother's lack of commitment to her child's activities and psychological well-being.

In addition to escorting children to the school gate in a properly laundered uniform each day, at least four times a week mothers were expected to awaken early in order to pack a nutritionally balanced and attractively prepared box lunch. Preparation of these boxes for family members of all ages approaches a folk art form in Japan, and many cookbooks and television cooking programs are devoted exclusively to methods of preparing them. The most important criteria, attractiveness and good nutrition, are believed to be met by supplying small amounts of many different types of foods.

In preschools these box lunches (*obentō*) assume a symbolic significance far beyond their nutritional value. In part, they represent a concrete manifestation of the mother's love and concern for the child and form a symbolic bond between the mother at home and the child at school. The director of Tokyo Preschool made these observations:

> *Obentō* are very important. By taking the trouble to make a nice lunch each morning, the mother communicates her feelings for her child. It's only during preschool that the mother will have this chance to get up a little early and do something nice for her child because when the child goes to elementary school, he'll have school lunch. It's also important that *obentō* be made especially for the child, not food left over from dinner or the adults' *obentō*. At home, mother prepares dinner according to what the father or older children like. The *obentō* is her chance to make something especially for that child and encourage his appetite. We ask mothers to prepare small quantities of three or four different cooked foods, plus fruit and rice, each

day. The flavoring of the foods should appeal to the child; most kids like all kinds of food rather sweet. It should be nutritious, be the kind of food children enjoy, look colorful, and be cutely prepared. When the child removes the lid of his lunch box at lunchtime, his mother's love and feelings for him should pop out of the box. Children should feel, "My mother made this just for me."

The director mentioned that the school had great difficulty in educating the occasional foreign mother who enrolled her child in the school about the importance of a proper *obentō*. With thinly veiled disappointment and pity, she related an incident that occurred when Tokyo Preschool invited the preschool class from a nearby international school on an excursion to a local park. She said that she and the other teachers were surprised when many of the foreign children unwrapped a stack of sandwiches "without even the crusts cut off" or brought "only an apple and a couple of chicken legs wrapped in aluminum foil rattling around in a brown paper bag." Tobin, Wu, and Davidson (1989) also describes the difference in American and Japanese expectations about what constitutes a properly prepared lunch.

Especially during the first several months of the school year, the proper preparation of *obentō* is the longest and most frequently repeated topic of discussion at monthly mothers' meetings, sometimes consuming up to thirty minutes of a one-hour meeting. These discussions do not focus on principles of nutrition in the Western sense or on actual techniques for turning apples into bunny rabbits or carrots into flowers. They focus primarily on how the food should be packed and wrapped and on which aspects of table manners should be inculcated at home and at school: boiled eggs, spaghetti, and rice that is not shaped into balls are difficult to eat and therefore are not to be included in the box; any food that is dropped on the floor should be deposited in the box lid rather than on the table; and so on.

Mothers are frequently encouraged to exert their best efforts in carefully preparing an attractive lunch and to think of the child eating the lunch as they prepare it. The preparation of *obentō* becomes both a primary symbol of the loving concern appropriate to the mother-child relationship and an important means of socializing Japanese mothers in participating in their child's school activities and demonstrating concern for his psychological well-being while away from home. Yet as we shall see later during the activities of the school day, the child's consumption of this *obentō*, prepared with love "just for him," involves a strict disciplining of indulgence in this *amae* symbol.

Besides readying the uniform and box lunch, mothers must equip their children each day with various small items. Mountain City Preschool was typical in requiring the mother to put a pocket handkerchief and a small packet of facial tissue in the uniform pocket and place the attendance record and the parent-teacher message book in the shoulder bag. In addition, a monthly schedule and occasional mimeographed sheets alert the mother to the proper day to send paint smocks, book bags, or judo clothes. Hand towels, indoor uniforms, and seat cushions are periodically sent home to be washed and must be returned to school on the correct day. Forethought and considerable preparation are needed to send a Japanese child to school properly equipped each day.

Special preparation of clothing and materials is required before the first day of preschool. Labels must be sewn or inked on each part of the school uniform, all accessories, and each piece of the child's regular clothing—all his outer clothing, underwear, socks, handkerchiefs, and overshoes. Every piece of equipment that the child uses at school also must be separately labeled, including each piece of the lunch box, the seat cushion, and each crayon. Mothers of newly enrolled students reported that they had to stay up late into the night for several days in a row to accomplish all this labeling.

Moreover, mothers are required to make numerous articles by hand. Although substitute items are available in stores, teachers asserted that children value handmade objects more highly and that the care with which the mother prepares and decorates these objects is an important demonstration of her affection. Tokyo Preschool was typical in insisting that the following items be made by hand according to specification by the end of the first month of preschool:

long-sleeved, button-down painting smock
cloth bag for modeling clay, lined with vinyl
appliquéd bag to take home monthly subscription magazines
    and books
wrapper for lunch box with velcro closure
drawstring bag for drinking cup
drawstring bag for toothbrush

special flame-retardant hooded cape, in case of fire (folded into a
zippered cushion and placed in the seat of the child's chair)

Each of these items represented a significant, even formidable,
sewing project. Nonetheless, all children appeared on the proper
day appropriately equipped. Furthermore, many had their items
beautifully embroidered or appliquéd in whimsical designs. This
investment of maternal energy indicates, if not Japanese mothers'
high degree of maternal affection and commitment, at least the
strength of each mother's desire not to appear as an unskillful
housewife in the eyes of the other mothers.

The very high expectations for maternal participation in Japanese preschools may be seen as an important influence in socializing Japanese mothers in their appropriate role in supporting their
children's education. Preschools reinforce maternal compliance
through frequent allusions to an assumed direct relationship between the strength of maternal love and the amount of maternal
assistance. They also provide numerous subtle opportunities for
mothers to compare each others' work.

At this stage in their child's school career, the mother is a novice
at assisting her child in school, just as her child is a novice in the
classroom. Principals and teachers often remind mothers of this
fact and of the importance of maintaining a serious attitude toward
the preschool's expectations. The phrase "Feel that you are also a
new student at this preschool" (*jibun mo nyūen shita tsumori de*) was
part of the principals' advice to the new mothers in both Tokyo
Preschool and Mountain City Preschool and is a standard part of
all advice to mothers of new students. By making clear its expectations in this regard and by requiring daily practice of supportive
behavior and attitudes, the preschool accustoms mothers to providing sustained, intensive support for the child's educational activities, which will be maintained throughout the child's school
career.

6

The Goals of Preschool Education

What are the primary goals of Japanese preschool education? Goals are reflected in sources as diverse as the official guidelines of the Ministry of Education, the attitudes and practices of teachers and principals, and mothers' own reasons for sending their children to preschool. The description of the goals takes different forms, from the academic wording of Ministry documents to the folk language of mothers discussing their own children. In this section I will examine the goals of preschool education from various social vantage points, showing that the primary aims of training children in appropriate social behavior and establishing fundamental habits of daily life hold for all groups within Japanese society.

OFFICIAL GOALS OF THE MINISTRY OF EDUCATION

The official preschool curriculum guidelines of the Ministry of Education, *Guidelines for Preschool Education,* were revised in April 1989. The previous guidelines dated from 1964 and were based on laws enacted in 1947. The 1989 revision constitutes primarily a shortening of the 1964 guidelines. The revised guidelines describe the goals of preschool education in section 2:

1. To cultivate the foundation of a sound body and mind through training the basic attitudes and habits [*kihonteki na seikatsu shūkan*] necessary for a healthy, safe, and happy life.

2. To develop affection for and confidence in other people and to cultivate the attitudes of independence [*jiritsu*], cooperation, and the seed of moral character.

3. To develop interest in and appreciation of nature and the phenomena around one, fine and wholesome sentiments [*yutaka na shinjo*] toward them, and understanding of them.

4. To develop interest in and appreciation of the words used in everyday life and to cultivate an attitude of pleasure in speaking and listening and a sense of the meaning of words.

5. To develop fine and wholesome sensibilities and an abundant imagination through a variety of personal experiences. (Monbu-shō 1989, 1–2)

Although phrased in general terms, these goals reveal several important characteristics of the official concept of Japanese preschool education. The primary goal of preschools is neither academic nor focused on preparing children for first grade. Rather, it is to provide a foundation of good character and develop a wholesome personality. This aim is accomplished through helping children establish good personal habits and attitudes and proper relationships with others. Mothers, as we have seen in previous chapters, enunciate similar goals—learning the meaning of life in a group (*shūdan seikatsu*) and basic habits of daily life (*kihonteki seikatsu shūkan*).

The 1989 guidelines specify five areas of content that are to form the instructional medium through which these goals are achieved: health, interpersonal relationships, the environment, language, and expression. The 1964 version listed six content areas: health, society, nature, language, music and rhythm, and arts and crafts. The revision has combined music and arts into the category "expression."

An inspection of the items within these five content areas shows that the primary objectives of developing good character and wholesome personality through good personal habits and proper social behavior are embedded throughout. For example, the first item under "health" is "to act vivaciously and freely and to know contentment" (*akaruku, nobi-nobi to kōdō shi, jujitsukan o ajiwau*). (To Westerners, this goal may seem more appropriate to a category such as "personality" than to "health.") Among the other items under "health" are "to be calm and stable in interactions with the teacher and students," "to acquire the routines of a wholesome daily life," and "to be able to keep one's things clean and accomplish dressing and undressing, eating, and elimination by oneself." Items under "interpersonal relationships" include "to do the things that one can for oneself," "to understand the fun of playing and working with other children," and "to realize that there are things one should not say or do when relating to others." Similarly, other content areas have items related closely to developing good interpersonal relationships and basic habits of daily life.

The term "basic habits of daily life" and its ubiquity as a goal of character training in preschool education stem from Japanese assumptions about the nature of ethical behavior. Good character and morality are driven by a person's beliefs and attitudes, and these are formed from the habitual residue of the personal habits and customs of daily life. The best way to develop good character and ethical behavior is to train oneself in its habits through attention to correct performance of daily routine. Children can acquire good character and ethical behavior through repeated practice in a conducive environment, and providing such an environment is one of the primary goals of the preschool curriculum.

Although expectations regarding the development of good character and personal relationships are high, those regarding reading and counting skills are surprisingly low. The 1989 guidelines note, "Systematic instruction in letters (*moji*) will begin after children enter elementary school. Therefore, in the preschool, children's interest, appreciation, and awareness of letters should be developed naturally and on an individual basis rather than through direct instruction" (Monbushō 1989, 8). Concerning numbers, the 1964 guidelines explicitly stated, "It is not desirable to purposelessly have children learn numerals or count large numbers of things." In the 1989 version this statement was modified: "Cultivate children's interest in and appreciation of quantity in a natural manner, carefully considering what the children themselves have experienced and actually find useful in their daily lives" (Monbushō 1989, 6).

Preschool and elementary-school teachers and principals unanimously agreed that the conventional rule for the upper limit of preschool instruction in letters and numbers is to teach children no more than to read and write their own name and to count as far as ten by the time they enter first grade. Although a few preschools make it a policy to exceed this criterion, they are comparatively rare.

A 1986 Monbushō survey of a random sampling of Japanese preschools asked in what manner instruction in letters and numbers was included within the curriculum. Thirteen percent reported providing whole-class instruction in letters to all students, and 8 percent did so in numbers. Seventy-two percent of the preschools chose the answer "The preschool environment is planned to provide various experiences and activities that naturally arouse interest in and appreciation of letters" as best describing their approach to teaching letters. Eighty-one percent chose a similar description of their instruction in numbers. Among the schools providing regular whole-class instruction in either subject, private schools were much more common than public ones (Monbushō 1986b, 40, 43).

Even though preschools reported that they did not regularly teach letters and numbers, most children do show considerable skill in these subjects. More than 90 percent of the schools noted that almost all of their students could read and write their names in phonetic letters (*kana*), recite numbers up to twenty, and correctly count ten objects. Roughly two-thirds of the schools reported that about half of their students could read simple storybooks in phonetic letters as well as spell simple words in phonetic letters (Monbushō 1986b, 42). Tobin, Wu, and Davidson (1989) and White (1987) indicate that much of this instruction is provided by mothers in the home.

Although the ministry's expectations regarding preschool instruction in basic reading and arithmetic are comparatively low, its expectations regarding music and dramatics have been comparatively high. The 1964 guidelines set as goals "to play instruments in part harmony and to change parts" and "to express what one has seen through theatrical activities." In all of the schools observed, the regular classroom teachers routinely trained the four- and five-year-olds to play simple tunes on various instruments, ranging from glockenspiels and snare drums to small, two-octave keyboard flutes.

At the cultural-activities festival held yearly in almost all Japanese preschools, it was common to see the entire student body play one or two simple tunes on percussion and keyboard instruments in part harmony and then to change parts. At these events each class also staged a musical skit or operetta. Students acted all of the roles, played some of the music, and made the costumes and scenery. The intensive rehearsals and preparations leading up to the festival provided six to eight weeks of intensive arts-related activity for the entire school.

Under the new category "expression" in the 1989 *Guidelines*, these goals are somewhat deemphasized. The item concerning music now reads, "to enjoy music and to know the pleasure of singing songs and using simple rhythm instruments." That for dramatics reads, "to express one's feelings through movement and words and to know the pleasure of dramatic play." Under this section the 1989 *Guidelines* notes "Children's naive and untutored (*sobokuteki*) expression of their own feelings should be preserved. One-sided instruction in artistic skills that is isolated from children's daily life should not occur" (Monbushō 1989, 9). It will be interesting to observe the future impact of these new guidelines on preschool cultural-activities festivals.

How do individual preschools translate the ministry's objectives into their own instructional program? The 1986 Monbushō survey asked preschools to characterize the relationship between their own instructional program and the six content areas of the ministry's 1964 objectives. Only 15 percent of the schools chose the answer "To ensure the full implementation of the Ministry's six content areas, each content area is reviewed as the basis for development of organized and systematic activities." Most schools approached the six content areas as general recommendations for enriching the play-centered, customary daily and yearly activities. Thirty-five percent chose the response "Play-centered activities form the nucleus of the program. Through the teachers' assistance with children's interests and experiences, the six content areas are covered in a general manner." Another 32 percent selected the answer "Situations and units are based on children's daily lives. Activities and experiences are chosen that relate to this and include the six content areas." Only 2 percent of preschools picked the response "In order to develop children's abilities, specific activities such as music, art, instruction in letters, physical education, etc., form the nucleus of instruction, with free play in between" (Monbushō 1986b, 32). It is clear that most preschools perceive their curriculum as focused on play and the regular routine of preschool life rather than regularized instruction.

The survey also asked preschools to choose the instructional objectives considered most important by their school. The two most commonly chosen objectives were "basic habits of daily life" and "a healthy body," each of which were selected by 71 percent of the schools. The other frequently cited objectives were "independence" (*jishu*, or doing one's own things for oneself), "kindness" (*omoiyari*), "wholesome sentiments" (*kansei no yutakasa*), and "social life" (*shakaisei*) (Monbushō 1986b, 55). As we shall see, these goals closely resemble the ones mothers describe for their children's preschool experience.

Teachers do have some latitude in translating the school's objectives into classroom activities. Most preschools report that daily instructional objectives are decided by the teacher. In planning weekly objectives, preschools are more evenly divided between those that determine them collectively and those that leave them to the teacher. Monthly and yearly objectives are usually jointly decided by the entire staff (Monbushō 1986b, 34).

Nonetheless, within the Japanese cultural context this discretion accorded teachers is understood to exist within the broad confines of precedent and custom for a particular school. For example, although schools report that the staff determines yearly objectives, in many schools the philosophy and yearly goals are set forth in a printed pamphlet that remains the same year after year. At the beginning of each school year the staff typically holds a short discussion to propose additions or changes, usually minor, to the established plan. Except in unusual cases, the result is mutual agreement that activities proceed according to custom. Similarly, at the classroom level the large body of custom and routine that makes up the Japanese preschool day accounts for all but a small amount of the discretion individual teachers have in planning daily classroom activities. The yearly calendar of the preschool includes at least one or two traditional activities for every month and a great deal of carefully observed daily routine. Furthermore, each Japanese teacher takes pains to ensure that her class's daily activities are not so unusual that they attract undue attention from other classes or break with established precedent and custom. A teacher may decide whether to have the children do origami or draw pictures on a given morning, but without extensive consultation with the director and other teachers she is unlikely to choose an activity that has never before occurred at the preschool.

INSTRUCTIONAL OBJECTIVES
OF MOUNTAIN CITY PRESCHOOL

How are the ministry's official guidelines reflected in the actual curriculum of a particular school? Although Mountain City is a

Buddhist preschool, its objectives bear a close resemblance to those of the secular schools studied as well as to the ministry's guidelines. An examination of Mountain City Preschool's month-by-month instructional objectives gives a clear indication of the strong emphasis on acquiring proper attitudes and social habits typical of the Japanese preschool curriculum.

Educational Objectives of Mountain City Preschool

Primary Objective: To realize that one is Buddha's child.
School Slogan: Vigorously, vivaciously, cooperatively.

First Semester Goal: Freely and easily [*nobi-nobi to*].

April: Be happy at starting preschool or entering the next higher grade. Become aware of oneself as a member of a group. Develop consideration for other people.
• Enjoy coming to preschool.
• Become able to perform the basic habits of daily preschool life.

May: Realize that there are rules and conventions in group life and that following them brings a happy life.
• Learn the fun of playing vigorously outdoors with other children.
• Follow the conventions of group life.
• Know the fun of participating in group activities.

June: Value one's own life as well as cultivate consideration for and a desire to preserve the life of all other living things.
• Take care of one's body.
• Be interested in nature's changes.
• Develop group consciousness.

July: Being kind to others makes one's own life happy. Understand that small acts of consideration brighten social life.
• Understand and follow the conventions of group life.
• Have confidence in and enthusiasm for preschool life.

Second Semester Goal: With a fine and wholesome heart [*kokoro yutaka ni*].

August: Try to do whatever one can for oneself. Willingly undertake even tasks which have not been assigned to one.
• Enjoy summer games and play.
• Deepen one's relationships with other children.

September: Nothing can be accomplished alone. Realize that we live by the blessings and assistance of society and nature.
• Acquire a self-reliant attitude.
• Be able to follow the rules of group activities.

October: By putting together the strength of many hands, unbelievably large tasks can be accomplished. Understand the joy and importance of working together.
• Satisfy interest in physical activity through exercise-related games.
• Taste the fun of cooperating with others through lively group activities.

November: Do not become discouraged in the middle but persevere until the end. The joy one feels after reaching the goal develops self-confidence.
• Take interest in nature as it appears in autumn.
• Enjoy expressive activity using natural objects.
• Have appreciation for the society around one.

December: Learn about Lord Buddha's teachings and realize that exerting one's best efforts toward realizing them brings a full and happy life.
• Pray that one may become a gentle, obedient, and diligent child.
• As it grows colder, appreciate the accompanying changes in daily life.

Third Semester Goal: Composure [*ochitsuki*].

January: Show a kind face and speak gentle words even when one feels pain or sadness.
• Enjoy winter games.
• Deepen one's relationships with other children.
• Persevere in work and thought until the end.

February: If one acts before thinking carefully, a mistake will be made. Communicate the importance of a calm and thoughtful life.
• Become a child who can bravely withstand the cold.
• Be able to express oneself confidently and in a lively manner.

March: Having dreams and aspirations is a happy way to live one's life. Understand the joy of working diligently toward those dreams.
• Have an independent daily life at preschool.
• Be mentally prepared for and look forward to promotion to the next higher grade.

With only minor changes in rhetoric and phrasing, most of the educational objectives of Mountain City Preschool are present in one form or another in the official guidelines of the Ministry of Education and in the objectives of the other preschools studied. Most of the items in the Mountain City objectives cover development of either proper personal habits and attitudes or cooperative social habits.

Some of Mountain City Preschool's objectives seem inconsistent.

Both reliance on the group and independence seem to be simultaneously stressed. For example, the goals for September are to learn that "nothing can be accomplished alone" but also to "acquire a self-reliant attitude." The August goals include "Try to do whatever one can for oneself," but in October one goal is "to understand the joy and importance of working together." In March children should learn to "have an independent daily life at preschool," but in April children are encouraged to "become aware of oneself as a member of a group." In fact, it is the difference between the American and Japanese interpretations of "independence," "self-reliance," and "doing what one can for oneself" that create the apparent inconsistency.

In the Japanese context, independence does not connote "going one's own way," social isolation, or personal autonomy. Applied to preschool children within the classroom environment, independence (*jishu*) and self-reliance (*jiritsu*) are the opposite of childish dependency and *amae*-based expectations of unnecessary assistance and indulgent attention from the teacher. To "try to do whatever one can for oneself" is the opposite of the child's expectation that others will do things for him. Although an American may read personal freedom and individualism into these words, for Japanese preschool teachers they refer almost exclusively to the need to have children learn to put aside their expectations of maternal assistance and assume responsibility for the activities required of them within the new world of *shūdan seikatsu*. For this reason, independence and self-reliance are cited as important habits for the Japanese child to cultivate in learning to become a member of a group.

Developing the right understanding of one's own tasks and responsibilities vis-à-vis the group and acquiring the habit of carrying out those responsibilities is the basis of Japanese preschool training in proper social attitudes and behavior. Learning proper habits of daily life (*kihonteki seikatsu shūkan*) means becoming accustomed to fulfilling automatically these social responsibilities.

We have seen that in the preschool, basic daily habits include changing clothes quickly and efficiently, looking after one's own belongings, using proper greetings and polite speech, and being cheerful and diligent. These abilities and attitudes all form the child's own portion of the social contract within the small society of the preschool, and fulfilling these responsibilities constitutes upholding one's own end of the social bargain. For this reason, the acquisition of proper daily habits is a prerequisite to full participation in society.

GOALS AND ASPIRATIONS OF MOUNTAIN CITY PRESCHOOL MOTHERS

Why do Japanese parents send their children to preschool? How do parents' goals for their children's preschool experience differ from or resemble those of the Ministry of Education and the typical preschool? During the maternal interviews, I asked sixteen mothers of new students at Mountain City Preschool, "By the time that your child finishes preschool, what do you hope he will have learned from the preschool experience?" and "What type of preschool student do you hope your child will become?" Because of the preponderance of boys among the new students at Mountain City Preschool, fourteen of the sixteen women interviewed were mothers of boys. Ten were mothers of incoming three-year-olds, and the other six were mothers of incoming four-year-olds. The mothers' responses fall into four major categories: relating well to others, controlling egoistic and regressive behavior, cheerfulness and robustness, and politeness and tractability.

The most common category of goals of Mountain City Preschool mothers for their children's preschool experience related to learning how to get along well with others. Every one of the mothers interviewed mentioned at least one goal in this area, and most mentioned two or three. Twelve of the sixteen mothers interviewed mentioned either "to become close to other children" (*tomodachi to nakayoku suru*) or "to develop good interpersonal relations" (*taijin kankei*). One-third of the mothers said they wanted their children to develop "kindness" (*omoiyari, yasashisa*), and another third mentioned "cooperation" (*kyōchōsei*). Other, less frequent responses assigned to this category were "to learn the rules of group life" and "to learn to behave the way everyone else does" (*mina to onaji koto o suru*).

The second category of goals Mountain City mothers most commonly mentioned for their children's preschool experience was to learn to control egoistic or regressive behavior. Five mothers chose as goals "to learn that one can't always have one's own way" (*jibun no omou bakari ni ikimasen*) or "not to push for one's selfish desires" (*wagamama o tōsenai*). Equally popular goals were to have children learn "endurance in the face of difficulty" (*gaman, nintai*) and "the difference between acceptable and unacceptable behavior" (*yatte ii, yatte wa ikenai koto no kubetsu*). More infrequent responses were "to take responsibility for one's own tasks" (*jibun no koto jibun de suru*) and "to listen to others' opinions before stating one's own" (*aitei no kimochi o kiite kara iu*).

The third most popular category of mothers' goals was to have their children develop a cheerful and robust personality. Within this category, half of the mothers desired that their child exhibit *genki*, a quality combining the concepts of good health, vigor, and cheerfulness. Other traits commonly desired were liveliness (*kappatsu, akarui*), and freedom and ease (*ōraka, nobi-nobi*).

Items in the first two categories, learning to get along well with others and learning to control egoistic and regressive behavior, were chosen frequently by mothers of both boys and girls. None of the mothers of girls, however, chose any items within the category of robustness and cheerfulness. Because there were only two mothers of girls in the sample, it is not possible to draw firm conclusions about gender differences, but this is an interesting topic for future investigation.

A less common category of goals for children's preschool experience was politeness and tractability. "To do what the teacher says" (*sensei no iu koto o kiku*), "to be easy to get along with" (*sunao*), and "to be able to greet others politely" (*aisatsu ga dekiru*) were each mentioned by two different mothers. It is interesting that this category was much less popular than that of cheerfulness and vigor. Being easy to get along with and obedient (*sunao*) is usually described as one of the most highly prized traits in Japanese children (Lebra 1976; White and LeVine 1986).

It is clear that Mountain City mothers were in basic agreement with the Ministry of Education that developing good character and a pleasing personality are the primary goals of the preschool experience. No mothers mentioned learning letter and number skills, drawing and singing, or anything related to the academic content of the preschool curriculum as a goal for their children. None mentioned even as broad a goal as "leaning about the world around them" as a reason for sending her child to preschool.

This is not to suggest, however, that Mountain City mothers were not interested in having their children learn to read and count. A separate section of the interview asked mothers about their child's abilities in this area. Each mother was able to describe in considerable detail her child's current level of knowledge and recalled incidents in which she informally encouraged it. Two mothers had already made some explicit attempt to teach their children to read. But Mountain City mothers overwhelmingly viewed preschool as a social rather than an academic learning environment.

To these mothers, the most important thing that preschool could teach their child about the world outside the home was the all-important lesson of how to relate well to other people and display the behavior appropriate to a group situation. It is clear, however, that they desired more for their children than merely to learn how to get along in a group. Mountain City mothers hoped that through the preschool their children would learn to sincerely enjoy the company of other children and have consideration for them. The responses "to be close to other children" (*tomodachi to nakayoku suru*), "to make a lot of friends," (*tomodachi o takusan tsukuru*), "consideration" (*omoiyari*), "kindness" (*yasashisa*), and "cooperation" (*kyōchōsei*) suggest that even at this early age Japanese mothers believe that social behavior should involve genuinely pleasant and caring relationships with a large number of children.

Exclusive friendships are not particularly encouraged among three- and four-year-olds. Instead, parents and teachers want children to develop a pleasant, cheerful, and cooperative relationship with all their schoolmates. Indeed, the very word "friend" (*otomodachi*) in Japanese preschool and elementary-school education is universally used to refer to all children, singly or collectively. By definition, all children whom a child knows are automatically friends, regardless of the degree of personal affinity or enmity. There is no separate word for the special persons Americans usually designate as friends, although sometimes the term "a friend one plays with often" (*yoku issho ni asobu tomodachi*) is used. In later chapters we shall see that this inescapable assumption of sociability and connectedness is an important part of the ethos of Japanese group life.

All parties to Japanese preschool education are in close agreement that the primary goal of the experience is to learn proper social attitudes and behavior. At Mountain City Preschool, however, mothers also tend to place emphasis on having their children learn to control egoistic behavior, whereas the guidelines of the Ministry of Education and the educational objectives of Mountain City Preschool stress acquiring basic habits of daily life. But in fact these are two different ways of describing the same thing. Properly performing basic tasks and discharging responsibilities of daily life in a self-reliant manner is predicated on the ability to control demanding and self-indulgent behavior. Mothers describe this objective in more colloquial, psychological terms, whereas the Ministry of Education expresses it more formally as habits to be acquired.

7

Daily Activities and Routines

The main curriculum of Japanese preschools is contained in the structure and routine of the school day itself. The objectives of training socially appropriate behavior and the habits and attitudes of group life are not accomplished through carefully planned curriculum units or extensive correction and disciplining of inappropriate behavior. Rather, they are nurtured through a gradual process of socialization in group routines and the inculcation of habits conducive to group life. The expectations and demands of the daily schedule and its attendant ritual are the main vehicle of instruction in this process.

Most Japanese preschools are in session between 235 and 239 days a year. This is slightly more than the thirty-nine week (234 days) minimum school year recommended by the Monbushō. Twenty-two percent of preschools exceed 239 days a year (Monbushō 1986b, 28). Preschools are in session six days a week, including Saturday. Children enrolled in preschool attend every day that it is in session, unless they are sick. Even in day-care centers Japanese parents do not send their children to preschool only on the days they work, as is sometimes the case in the United States.

The 1986 Monbushō survey asked preschools to choose the seven activities or experiences to which they attached the most importance. The seven most commonly chosen, in descending order of popularity, were activities using rotated monitors (*tōban*) to carry out certain duties (55 percent of the preschools), annual Sports Day (46 percent), pretend play (44 percent), sand play (43 percent), making things (41 percent), picture books (34 percent), and cultivating plants (31 percent) (Monbushō 1986b, 39).

Other activities chosen as important by at least one-fifth of the preschools were playing with balls, playing in a swimming pool, sharing time (*seikatsu happyōkai*), talking with friends, playing with seeds, leaves, and insects, and all school assemblies (*shūkai*). These activities are typical of virtually all Japanese preschools, even if they are not among the seven considered most important by any particular preschool.

The broad outline of a typical day at Mountain City Preschool is almost identical to the daily rituals described by Tobin, Wu, and Davidson (1989) and Hendry (1986) in the preschools they visited. In some cases, the activities and routines are explicitly designed to accomplish stated social objectives. In others, training is more subtle and indirect. Occasionally the relationship between social objectives and daily routines is present only at the subconscious level of cultural habit and therefore is noticeable primarily to the outside observer.

To better understand Japanese preschool life, several preliminary generalizations should be made. First, Japanese preschools strive to avoid being teacher-centered. As Tobin, Wu, and Davidson note (1987), this decentering is both a conscious goal and an outgrowth of the comparatively large number of students in each class. Teachers are slow to assert direct authority or give instructions unless absolutely necessary (Lewis 1984). Children are encouraged to rely on each other as much as possible for routine behavior correction and for direction of class activities.

Second, activities in Japanese preschools are much less oriented toward formal academic instruction than is the case in American preschools. Harold Stevenson and colleagues in Japan did a time-sampling study of four randomly chosen hours of children's activities in the classes of five-year-olds at twenty-four preschools in Sendai and the same number of schools in Minneapolis (Stevenson 1987). They found that the preschoolers in Sendai were directly instructed 5 percent of the time, compared to 20 percent of the time in Minneapolis. The Japanese children were engaged in free play 25 percent of the time, as opposed to 12 percent of the time in the United States.

Reflecting the Japanese emphasis on social interaction between children, preschoolers in Sendai were smiling at or touching each other in 70 percent of the spot observations, in comparison with only 40 percent of the observations in Minneapolis. Japanese children were talking to each other in 80 percent of the observations, and in only 50 percent of the observations in the American preschools. The Stevenson study thus shows Japanese preschools to be more socially oriented, play-centered environments than are American ones.

Third, Japanese adults in general, and preschool teachers in particular, remain comfortable and unconcerned despite extremely high levels of children's noise and unrestrained activity. At Mountain City Preschool, on cold and rainy winter days when 60 children must play in the four small classrooms, even shouted conversations between adults often became inaudible. On such days teachers tacitly invited the noise by encouraging the children to remove the rhythm and percussion instruments from storage and by setting up the trampoline. Similarly, during play periods throughout the year no attempt was made to restrain children's motor activity. Children were not admonished for dancing on desk tops, climbing on and hanging from room partitions, or playing shrieking games of tag through the crowded rooms.

Although the noise level of the indoor play periods left this American observer with a headache and a feeling of disorientation, Japanese teachers considered it a positive phenomenon. On such days the children were described as *genki* (healthy, vigorous) and the noisy, sweaty, breathless play as *kodomorashi* (refreshingly childlike). Rather than ensuring that noise and activity never climb beyond a moderate level, Japanese preschools prefer to take an all-or-nothing approach.

Many times each day, the tempo and tenor of activity fluctuates between a tight and a loose structure. Chaotic periods of free play are followed by silent, formal ritual. In Japanese preschools the measure of good discipline is not an overall low level of noise and controlled activity but a quick and precise maintenance of the boundaries between two radically different levels of order. If an observer does not understand this, the same Japanese preschool may be characterized as either quasi-military in discipline or totally chaotic and unrestrained.

The Japanese consider the ability to recognize what type of behavior is appropriate at a given moment and to make an efficient and orderly transition to that level of activity to be a crucial classroom habit and a basic social skill. Being able to come to order (*kiritsu ga dekiru*) quickly and efficiently in the classroom is the forerunner of the more mature ability to understand distinctions (*kejime ga wakaru*). Properly observing the distinctions among the behaviors appropriate to various situations is a basic component of Japanese ethics.

The beginning and end of each daily activity typically involves a brief formal ritual, during which the children stand in assigned places, assume a predetermined and immobile body position, and recite or sing in unison a brief, situationally appropriate expression of sentiments. Following the teacher's patterned response, the atmosphere relaxes, and the primary activity begins. During the activity itself, although participation is encouraged, children often wander away from the group or even out of the classroom if they lose interest. At end of the activity the teacher laboriously recalls the children to resume their places so that the formal concluding ritual can be performed.

ARRIVING AT PRESCHOOL

Each morning, the teachers are the first to reach the preschool, usually arriving between 8:00 and 8:30 A.M. While busily opening the shutters, heating water for tea, and organizing the day's materials, they laugh and chat amicably. Children begin arriving at preschool between 8:30 and 9:00 A.M., hand in hand with their mothers or riding in a child's seat on the back of mother's bicycle. Teachers then move to the school yard or entrance foyer to greet the arriving children and their mothers.

Proper greetings are an important part of the Japanese preschool curriculum. The Ministry of Education's official guidelines state that one of the objectives of language learning is "to make everyday greetings in a friendly way" (Monbushō 1989, 6). The principal of Mountain City Preschool, in his opening-day remarks, cited "becoming a child who can greet others correctly" (*aisatsu no dekiru kodomo ni naru*) as one of the school's main objectives.

A polite greeting is more than a smile of welcome or a friendly hello. A proper greeting must follow a ritual format. As child and mother come within speaking distance of the teacher in the morning, they make the first move. Coming to a full halt with both feet together and hands in front, child and mother bow, inclining their heads from three to six inches, and loudly announce, in standard formal language, *sensei, ohayō gozaimasu* (good morning, Teacher). The child has now "officially" arrived at school. The teacher smiles in recognition and returns the greeting and bow, saying *ohayō go-zaimasu* to the mother and child collectively.

Most children do not perform their part of the greeting ritual properly. They either ignore the greeting and continue walking or stand silently looking at the ground. Mothers and teachers explain that this behavior is due to "shyness." Both mother and teacher then spend several moments cajoling and encouraging the child to say good morning until he either makes a recognizable response or escapes by running off to the classroom. Most children remain too "shy" to spontaneously executive a properly polite response until they are six or seven years old. (See page 103 for a verbatim transcript of a mother and teacher attempting to get a child to make proper greetings.)

The child then proceeds to the classroom to put away his belongings and change clothes. After removing and hanging up his traveling smock, shoulder bag, and traveling hat, he puts on his play smock and play hat. When he has stacked his parent-teacher message book on the teacher's desk, he is free to run about and play. After three to six months of school, children become able to accomplish this transition quickly and efficiently, with virtually no assistance from the teacher.

Changing into appropriate clothing and organizing materials immediately on arrival is one of the many basic habits of daily life that Japanese preschools take great pains to inculcate in students. The habits will be further elaborated in elementary school and will remain with the children throughout adult life. Changing clothes on arrival at school or work reinforces the symbolic distinction between the outside world and the group life of the institution and ensures that all participants are properly organized for the activities of the day.

MORNING PLAY PERIOD

The morning play period lasts from the time the child has finished changing clothes and organizing his belongings until roughly 10:00 A.M. At Mountain City Preschool, children are encouraged to play outdoors during all seasons and in all weather except heavy rain. This policy is consonant with the ministry's objective for health instruction, "to play outdoors as much as possible."

Indigenous Japanese medical theories hold that children become more healthy and vigorous if their bodies are consistently exposed to the cold. Withstanding cold is believed to strengthen the character and "improve the circulation." To this end, most preschools and elementary schools urge parents to dress their children lightly. A few go so far as to have children go barefoot and wear only shorts during the summer, adding a T-shirt during the winter. Mountain City Preschool was typical of most preschools in that mothers dressed children in warmer fabrics and thick hose during the winter, but the regulation uniforms included shorts or short skirts the year around.

Although office buildings and adult workplaces are typically comfortably heated during the winter, preschools and elementary schools have only the most rudimentary heating. In Mountain City, where winter daytime temperatures are rarely above freezing, temperatures in the classrooms are usually 55–60° Fahrenheit. Despite the cold, wearing coats in the classroom is not permitted, and during playtime wearing coats and mittens outdoors is frowned on. This regime is believed to increase children's ability to endure hardship as well as strengthen their resistance to respiratory infections. In this way Mountain City Preschool attempts to provide an environment in which children learn "not to become discouraged but to persevere until the end" and "to become able to withstand the cold bravely," as stated in the preschool's educational objectives.

Children of all ages and both sexes enjoy playing on the swings, jungle gym, and bars. When it rains, the center of the playground becomes a four- to five-inch-deep puddle in which boys and girls wade joyfully in rubber boots, probing about with sticks. During the winter months, when the puddle freezes, the children "skate" in their boots or chip away at the corners of the ice. Except during the coldest part of the winter, the most popular activity at play period for most of the three-year-olds is water play in the sandy dirt, digging ditches, building roads, and making mud pies. Because scoops, buckets, molds, and dishes are intentionally in short supply, energetic builders must spend considerable time negotiating with others to borrow or maintain the equipment they need. Aside from negotiations of varying degrees of friendliness over equipment, most three-year-olds play in a solitary but companionably parallel manner.

Four- and five-year-olds play much more socially, often informally separating themselves by sex. Girls play together at cooking mud pies and holding tea parties or play house indoors, improvising tiny homes from dolls, blocks, and scarves. Instigated by the leaders among the five-year-olds, they also play traditional line and circle singing games, such as *kagome, kagome* and *hana ichi monme*. Small groups of girls huddle together, chatting and planning secrets, holding hands, and giggling. The more officious five-year-olds also frequently swoop down to "help" and coo over the smaller and slower-moving of the three-year-olds.

Boys enjoy playing with cars and trucks and building roads in the sandy dirt. Running, shouting, and mock dueling games are also extremely popular. Although a generation ago small Japanese boys may have imitated the swordfighting of samurai warriors, modern Japanese boys carefully study and imitate the heroes of their favorite children's television shows. "Dynaman," "Ultraman," and "Robokko" wear flashy futuristic uniforms and bulky protective gear. They are armed with an eclectic arsenal of flimsy but symbolically fearsome hand weapons, such as light beams, rubber hatchets, and magical chains. After a long windup of ritualized posturing and stylized shouts, a single touch of the hero's weapon causes the strongest of enemies to fall dead with a crash. The hero then proclaims his victory with another set of ritualized postures and shouts. When this game is played by children, the actual physical contact involves no more than a mild "karate chop," usually preceded by a breathless chase until the quarry is cornered for the ritual windup and "death blow."

Boys tirelessly practice imitating their favorite's fighting style. Teachers regard their exaggerated posturings and make-believe fights with humor, praising their spontaneous demonstrations of shadowboxing with such exclamations as "skillful" (*jōzu*) and "great form" (*kakkō ii*). When challenged to a duel, most teachers can execute a surprisingly competent routine themselves.

Teachers do not regard these make-believe fights as aggression, or the warlike posturing and stylized shouts as indicative of violent tendencies. They are seen as age- and sex-appropriate games and as a legitimate means of social interaction. Even when an unsuspecting victim receives a sudden "death blow" from behind, teachers ignore the irritated counterwallop or brief bout of surprised and indignant tears. In the only observed instance where a teacher intervened in such a situation, she merely asked the sniffling victim, "I wonder if Tetsuya [the would-be Dynaman] wants to play?"

Social interaction of all types is important. Lewis (1984) has also noted that play periods are sometimes arranged so that materials are in short supply. This practice is believed to promote interaction and make children learn to work together. Never is the number of children allowed to use a particular toy or play area predetermined or limited. Often children are shoulder to shoulder in the most popular play areas and activities. This lends a quality of mild confusion and noisy good cheer Japanese approvingly describe as *nigiyaka*. A *nigiyaka* preschool is considered a happy place to be.

Even fights and disagreements are positive indications of the gradual maturation of social interaction and genuine interpersonal involvement. Japanese teachers believe that through childish disputes children come to learn the proper boundaries between themselves and others. As Lewis (1984) has beautifully described in her study of cooperation and control in Japanese nursery schools, fights and other incidents that occur during playtime are often used as material for class discussions. Children are encouraged to express their feelings and ideas about the incidents that have taken place. In a properly cooperative group atmosphere the details of children's fights, games, and personal discoveries are all considered common property and are treated as problems or accomplishments of the entire group.

"Problem" children are those who consistently remain by themselves. A child who remains indoors alone during play period to look at books or experiment alone on the piano soon finds a teacher at his side deftly redirecting him outdoors to join a group of children. In response to a query about how teachers should handle children who honestly prefer quiet solitary pursuits to the collective enthusiasm of the playground, the veteran director of Tokyo Preschool confidently replied that in all her experience she had never met a child who truly preferred solitary activities; there were only "those who had not yet discovered how much fun it is to play with others."

The Japanese teacher's approach to children during play period is not that of a playground supervisor. As Lewis (1984) notes, preschool children often play completely unsupervised for long periods of time while teachers interact with children in other areas of the building or grounds, answer the telephone, or prepare the day's activities. Teachers are not particularly suspicious or fearful of what children are doing when out of their sight. Beyond having a teacher available somewhere in the building, the staff feels no need to provide constant supervision. Falls, fights, and misdemeanors, if not eventually handled by the children themselves, become the substance of later group discussions and learning experiences.

When teachers are present on the playground, they interact with the children. The image so familiar to Americans of a watchful playground supervisor standing alone in a corner of the yard or talking with a small group of children is rare in Japan. In fact, an observer scanning a Japanese preschool yard will almost always find the teacher squatting or in motion, playing or helping the children. It is frequently stated in the professional literature for preschool teachers that they should squat down when speaking with children to meet them at eye level.

Teachers interact with children at play nondirectively, serving primarily as a supportive and appreciative audience. They "eat" countless mud pies prepared by the little girls and zoom trucks along sandy roadways. Their professional role is not described as creatively guiding the child's play to stimulate intellectual discovery or catalyze social interaction. Instead, their role is to help children wholeheartedly engage in play as an end in itself.

Yōji to hoiku (Children and Child Care), the preeminent monthly professional magazine for Japanese preschool and day-care teachers, frequently offers teachers advice about play. These excerpts are from a typical article titled "Helping Children Become Accustomed to Preschool and Play," written by the staff of the journal:

Allow Children to Enjoy Sufficiently the Games They Choose Themselves

Play brings enjoyment and satisfaction in itself; it is not something of which the teacher should expect an outcome or effect. Children initiate play of their own volition, therefore it brings the satisfaction of self-realization. The sparkle in the eyes of a child at play is a wonderful thing. A child who has begun to play at an activity of his own invention deserves the teacher's respect. . . .

How nice it is to be a teacher who can resonate in sympathy with the joy children feel in their play. Such a teacher is of lasting assistance to the child's development. The teacher's responsibility toward a child who has begun to play is to judge accurately the child's situation. Sometimes children need to be approached. For example, to a child who drops a tricycle to move to a different game the teacher should say, "Let's put the tricycle in the garage, okay?" For a child who sits uninvolved, fingering a toy, it's important to help the child understand the fun of playing with that toy. The teacher's responsibility is to develop a knack for giving the amount of support appropriate to each individual child. (April 1983:51)

Japanese preschool teachers value spontaneity and whole-hearted engagement in childlike play. During the play period children are allowed to play as they like, with minimal adult intervention. Although friendly social play is preferred to fights or solitary pastimes, teachers try to provide an environment in which the child will develop these socially appropriate preferences naturally. Children's enjoyment of social activities should not be the result of an anxious or conscious attempt to conform to the teacher's limits and expectations. The long-term goal of social interaction is the acquisition of an intuitive understanding and acceptance of the limits of give and take inherent in group life. The play period is structured to facilitate this objective.

Japanese society eventually expects a high degree of self-control and suppression of personal desires and feelings in public social situations. But the wish to assume this control must be initiated and sustained by the child himself, or else, it is believed, the long-term effectiveness of the child's social adjustment will be impaired. For this reason, teachers are unruffled by demonstrations of selfish or regressive behavior, preferring that a child who has not yet developed an understanding of proper behavior straightforwardly express his feelings rather than attempt an artificial form of behavior beyond his level of genuine understanding.

The authenticity of children's natural enthusiasm is prized and must not be unduly suppressed in the socializing process. Unrestrained activity and noisy, joyful play are therefore highly valued. Noisy enthusiasm and joy are the naive expressions of eagerness and motivation (*iyoku*). An experienced teacher at one of the elementary schools in Mountain City made these insightful observations about the relationship between childish enthusiasm, *iyoku,* and later character strength:

From a teacher's point of view, "good," well-behaved children [*ii ko*] are much easier to deal with. They do just what you tell them and don't get in the way. But they have no real excitement and enthusiasm in their hearts, and that's not good for the child in the long run. In preschool and early elementary school it's a mistake to cut the childlikeness and enthusiasm out of the child. Although by chopping off their excitement when it's troublesome you can get a well-mannered student, this will be a great waste in the end. Enthusiasm [*iyoku*] is very important. If a child loses this, he won't have the strength to undertake things on his own [*jihatsusei*] later. If you watch children when they are at play, you can see what they're really like. The children who are always so full of energy they can't be bothered by what the teacher says and don't mind if they get in trouble are strong. The ones who are careful, always do things just right, and don't get right in there with the rest of the kids are weak. That's because they don't have honest enthusiasm, which comes from their hearts. Maybe they didn't play enough in a wholehearted way with other children when they were small. Enthusiasm is a strength that gives power to one's life, in everything one does. As a teacher, it's one's responsibility to help the children who are too "good" and too careful to lose their constricted feeling and revive their enthusiasm.

The goal of the play period is not to stimulate intellectual or social development through guided play. Rather, its main goal is to foster enjoyment of play for its own sake, and its secondary goal is to provide experience in social interaction. Teachers believe that these objectives must be achieved at the child's own pace, through natural, spontaneous interaction in a conducive environment. Teachers encourage children to express their natural enthusiasm and childlikeness freely, whatever the level of noise or activity that results.

TRANSITION: CLEANUP
AND SETTING UP THE ROOM

The play period draws to a close as teachers quietly remark to the children around them that it is time to start picking up the toys. The news and cleanup activity gradually spread, and teachers move about, encouraging individual children and assisting with the more complicated cleanup jobs. Until the children become able to pick up the school yard and classroom on their own, teachers assume an active role in cleanup. They neither organize the task (such as by calling for volunteers to pick up the sandbox) nor do much of the work themselves. Instead, they focus on children who are not assisting in the process. Transcripts of teachers' speech during cleanup period show a large number of direct requests: "There are still some things out here, Sato-chan, please pick them up"; "Put these in here"; "Masato, what are you doing? Pick this up."

As the toys are picked up, children who feel the need wash their hands and use the toilet. Others pull the tables and chairs out from the wall and set them up in the middle of the room. For the first several weeks, when children are learning how to perform this activity, teachers assume an active role: "Please help bring out the chairs"; "Where should you put the table?"; "Where does this chair go?"; "Just one of these is enough."

As children become more adept at setting up the room, teachers gradually withdraw almost completely from the setting-up process. In classrooms at all levels of Japanese education, setting up and preparing the room for scheduled activities is the job of the students rather than the teacher. Usually, the teacher formally arrives and begins the lesson after this step is completed.

Learning to accomplish tasks as a group, without a delegation of roles or a division of labor, is an important part of what the Ministry of Education means by the objective "to work and play together happily with friends." The give and take involved in the process of mutual participation is as important as the accomplishment of the task itself. Rather than stepping in to organize the activity efficiently and delegating children to perform specific tasks, Japanese teachers prefer to allow children to learn how to organize themselves and work together, even at the expense of extra time and some confusion.

MORNING GREETINGS

As soon as the room is set up, the teacher begins to play a melody at the piano, the signal for the students to hurry to their seats. This melody is the same every day of the year, and also the same in all classes in a given school. Once everyone is seated, the music changes to the introduction to the morning hello song. At this signal all children sit straight, with their hands on their knees and both feet on the floor, and the class sings in unison the school's hello song.

The hello song expresses optimistic, virtuous, and situationally appropriate sentiments. Tokyo Preschool's song is typical:

> On the wide playground
> Underneath the shining sun
> Little flowers lift their laughing face.
> Beneath the spreading branches

Of the old pine tree,
Lots and lots of friends have come.
Let's play together happily
All day long.

After the song the children recite in chorus, "Good morning, Teacher, good morning, everyone," bowing in turn to the teacher and fellow classmates. In the moment of silence that follows, the teacher replies, "Good morning, everyone," and immediately begins the five- to seven-minute period of morning announcements. This is the first time during the day that the teacher addresses the class as a whole. Until this moment all remarks have been addressed to individuals, and all transitions have been managed indirectly, through the prearranged signals such as a specific piano melody.

During morning announcements the teacher briefly describes the plan for the day. In some preschools, this activity includes calling the roll and having each child answer *hai* (yes). In others, two monitors (*tōban*) are designated from the roster and lead the class in reciting "Today is Monday. The weather is sunny." At this time spontaneity and unrestrained activity are completely inappropriate. It is a formal, public moment, and children are expected to stand or sit at attention, listen silently, and sing loudly, vigorously expressing the appropriate sentiments. This formality is termed "coming to order" (*kiritsu suru*).

In all preschools, this period is much more formally conducted than the activities preceding or following it. The sequence of topics is unvarying. The language is formal, movements are ritualized, and sentiments are strictly limited to the situationally appropriate. Children act or speak only in unison or in predetermined order, and both teacher and students attempt to remain carefully within their roles. No attempt is made to liven up the presentation or change the pattern from time to time to induce variety. In fact, the goal is to follow the pattern as closely as possible.

Mastering the behavior appropriate to such formal, collective greeting rituals is an important habit of daily life in Japanese society. Public events of all types, from committee meetings to wedding receptions, begin similarly. Following a formalized positioning of the body, there is a solemn, conventional exchange of greetings and recitation of polite, situationally appropriate, and optimistic sentiments. This ritual is part of observing *kejime*, which requires clear-cut distinctions in the behavior, style of speech, and expression of sentiment appropriate to various situations.

MORNING ACTIVITY PERIOD

At about 10:30 A.M., immediately following the announcements, a thirty- or forty-five-minute group activity period begins. The specific nature of the activity varies from day to day, but invariably it involves the entire class. Activities requiring desks and paper are common, such as doing origami, drawing pictures, or making materials for upcoming school projects. At Mountain City Preschool mimeographed worksheets with letter, number, or word activities are never used.

The pace and instructional style of the activity period is considerably more relaxed than that of morning greetings, and children are rarely cautioned about inappropriate behavior. Although children are encouraged to participate, and instructions or remarks are addessed to the class as a whole, those who lose interest are allowed to move about the classroom and even to wander out of the room. Children talk excitedly and call back and forth to each other freely during the activity.

The activity period transcribed from field notes below occurred during the tenth month of school in Mountain City Preschool's class of three-year-olds. The nature of the activity, the style in which it was taught, and the children's behavior are typical of activity periods in the other preschools observed.

The teacher announces, "We're going to make balloons from origami paper," and holds up a sample. "Who knows how to make a balloon already?" Children call out and talk excitedly, some raising hands. "Those who want yellow paper come and get it." Some students come to get paper and return to their seats. Raising her voice over the sounds of children moving about and chattering, the teacher calls, "Those who want green paper, come and get it." In this manner she goes through each of the five colors of paper available, one at a time, until all students have come to receive their preferred color of paper from the teacher and have returned to their seats.

The teacher calls out over the general noise of children relaxing and chatting with each other, "Put the white side up," holding up her own paper for the children to see. "Fold it in a rectangle." Some children call, "Teacher, I know how to do this already!" Another bounces a finished balloon. The teacher says, "Those who know how should go ahead and make theirs." Some children set to work enthusiastically, chatting with their friends while they complete their balloons.

The teacher holds up the rectangle, asking, "Has everyone made a rectangle?" She looks around the classroom. "Next fold it into a square. Iron the corners nicely." She pauses and looks around. "Next it's a little tricky. Open the square and fold the corners into the middle like this." She demonstrates, but the sample is so small that it's hidden in her hands, and the folds are so complex that even the observer is lost. "Can you do it?" Surprisingly, some of the children can. The teacher goes from desk to desk, fixing each child's work in turn. This process takes about five minutes.

As the teacher moves around the room, the children relax and chat, some playing with their neighbors. Several get up and begin to write on a portable blackboard; one takes out blocks and begins to play. The noise level is high, and everyone is relaxed, including the teacher. Among the children who have begun other activities are those who have finished their balloons and those who have lost interest in the task.

The teacher comes back to the center of the room, asking, "Has everyone got that?" Holding up her own piece, she demonstrates. "Now make it like a mountaintop and fold it like this. Fold it nice and straight." She again moves from desk to desk. As more and more of the children begin to abandon their half-finished work to wander about and play, the teacher calls, "Those who've gotten that far, wait a minute." Two or three of the children have already left the classroom to play on the playground.

The teacher returns to the front of the room and demonstrates the last two steps, including blowing up the finished balloon. "Can you do all this?" She begins to assist individual children again, and as each child finishes, he stands up and begins to bounce and bat his balloon excitedly. The teacher calls, "You can all take these home." Soon almost the entire class is at play, and many have moved out to the playground. The teacher remains at the desks, helping the last children complete their balloons.

After everyone is finished, the teacher chats with three girls who remain behind, folding various other origami figures. She shows one of them how to make a penguin, and for the rest of the period children continue to play as they like, until it is time to clean up for lunch.

LUNCH

At about 11:45 A.M. the teacher remarks to the children near her that it is almost time for lunch. Children pick up the toys and materials used during the activity period, encouraged by the teacher's instructions. They are supposed to use the toilet, if necessary, and wash their hands before readying their things for lunch.

Eating lunch entails a surprisingly complex ritual. The preschool's expectations for eating behavior are particularly high, in the light of the informal and mother-dependent eating habits to which most of the children are accustomed at home. As lunchtime approaches, each child takes his lunch box from his shoulder bag and removes it and its accompanying equipment from its special drawstring bag. He must then arrange the box, chopsticks, and other assorted pieces properly on the desk in front of him.

First, the child unfolds a special handkerchief that serves as a placemat and lays it on the desk. He removes the chopsticks from their box and places them horizontally in front of him. He removes the cup from its bag and puts at the upper right, then replaces the chopstick box and the cup bag in the drawstring bag and stores it on the shelf underneath the table. Next, he sets the lunch box inside its lid and places it in the center of the handkerchief. The monitors for the day pour weak tea or pass out milk, which is placed at the top of the arrangement. After finishing their rounds, the monitors come to stand beside the piano.

As each child finishes his preparations, he sits with his hands on his knees and his neatly arranged lunch box open before him, waiting for his classmates to make ready. It normally takes from five to ten minutes for the entire class to finish in the toilet and complete preparations. With delicious smells filling the room and their mother's tempting bites of food spread before them, children must now wait with hands in their laps for the signal to begin.

The teacher waits until every child is seated properly and the class is quiet. Then she nods to the monitors, who lead the class in singing the lunchbox song to her piano accompaniment:

> It's lunch time! It's lunch time!
> How happy we all are!
> Our little hands are bright and clean.
> Let's eat with hearty appetite,
> And chew each mouthful well.
> Without spilling or dropping food,
> Let's finish every bite.

After the song and before starting to eat, the class recites in unison a longer version of the polite formula used before meals in Japan:

Teacher, I'm going to eat [*sensei, itadakimasu*].
Everyone, I'm going to eat [*minasan, itadakimasu*].

Children eat in different ways. Some quickly finish the entire contents of their lunch box; others eat slowly, with long soliloquies between bites or brief trips to examine their friends' lunch boxes. Some children handle their chopsticks well; others spill almost as much as they manage to put in their mouths. Teachers eat quickly and quietly, then move about the room, encouraging children who have difficulty eating all of their food to take at least a few more bites. Finishing one's meal brings praise.

After finishing lunch, each child is expected to incline his head briefly and recite *gochisōsama deshita* (it was good), another polite mealtime formula. As most children forget to do this, the teacher habitually reminds those she sees preparing to leave the table, "Did you say *gochisōsama?*" In some preschools children must wait at their places until most of the class is finished, at which point they recite *gochisōsama deshita* in unison.

After the meal children must rewrap each piece of their equipment, stow them all in the drawstring bag, and replace it in their shoulder bag. They then get their toothbrush from the collection in a cup by the classroom sink and brush their teeth with water. Many use the chance to gargle ostentatiously. While the slowest children finish their lunches, others play here and there about the classroom or go outside to play.

Lunch is a significant part of the preschool curriculum. It is much more than merely a chance to eat or even to chat socially with friends. It constitutes a valuable lesson in basic daily habits and the customs of Japanese group life. Much of the training focuses on the etiquette of eating. However, the aspects of etiquette emphasized are for the most part not what Americans classify as table manners, such as holding the utensils properly or keeping the left hand out of the food. Instead, training in Japanese preschools focuses on the social aspects of eating behavior, such as performing preliminary rituals, remembering to begin and end the meal with the appropriate polite formulas, and adjusting one's eating speed to that of one's companions. Children who eat slowly are urged to try to finish their lunch by the time their classmates do, and those who finish early are encouraged to remain at the table to wait for their friends.

In Japan, eating together is an important occasion for social interaction. A great deal of care is taken to ensure that each person eats identical food, so that mutuality and common preferences are affirmed. In preschool the social expectation that everyone will eat the same food coexists with the notion of the daily lunch box as a unique, personal link between the mother at home and the child at preschool. Conflicts arising between the simultaneous desires for uniformity and personalization probably contribute to the extraordinary amount of attention focused in mothers' meetings on exactly what types of food are and are not to be included, how the food is to be shaped, and how the lunch box is to be wrapped and equipped.

Similarly, the issue of food preferences is at the juncture of two conflicting social expectations. The 1964 *Guidelines* of the Ministry of Education set forth as an educational objective "to acquire proper eating habits and not to have likes and dislikes regarding food." This goal was echoed by all preschool teachers and principals interviewed. The same authorities, however, urged mothers to arise early each day to prepare special children's foods for the lunch box to suit the child's taste, molding the portions as cutely as possible. Such special indulgence is not believed to encourage children's picky or demanding eating behavior. Instead, the extra time a mother spends preparing the lunchbox betokens her indulgent love for and desire to please her child.

Once at preschool, however, the consumption of this meal becomes hedged about with rules that defer or deny gratification of the *amae* symbol. First, children must wait to eat their food, sitting hungry for at least five minutes, with their hands on their knees and the lunch box open, until the entire class is ready. By contrast, mothers report that at home they schedule mealtimes according to the child's appetite. At home most preschool children are allowed to eat as soon as they arrive at the table, without waiting for the rest of the family and usually without the ritual *itadakimasu*. Most children are also allowed to refuse to come to the table if they are not hungry.

Furthermore, in preschool, children are expected to eat all of their food. Likes and dislikes are to be overcome. Many preschools request the mother to put in the lunch box each day one small piece of a food the child dislikes, properly masking it, by combining it with an appealing food; for instance, she may disguise spinach by turning it into a spinach egg roll. At school, teachers then urge the children to eat everything in their lunch boxes.

Preschool teachers have several ways of cajoling reluctant children to eat. Children are told that the food in question is delicious and that they should try a little bit. They are also frequently told that it will help them grow strong and tall. If these methods do not work, they are sometimes admonished, "And here your mother went to the trouble of making it just for you."

Lunchtime at preschool thus is similar to other aspects of the daily schedule in that children must learn to cope by themselves with tasks that are performed for them by their mothers at home. Moreover, they must learn to perform the activity in conformance with proper social behavior and etiquette. Lunchtime is unique, however, in that it does not require a radical break with the *amae*-based world of the home. Rather, the child brings to school a powerful symbolic representation of that *amae* but finds he must learn to discipline and control carefully his gratification from that object. Lunchtime therefore can be considered symbolic of the shaping of the *amae*-based feelings of the home in the direction of greater self-discipline and social acceptability.

Another aspect of the group training that occurs during lunch is lessons in neatness and tidiness in managing equipment and belongings. In both traditional and contemporary Japanese educational settings, each piece of equipment has its proper way of being arranged and used as well as its own case or container. Learning to manage these many pieces properly and efficiently is necessary when entering any new learning environment or workplace. In preschool the two most important examples are training in arranging one's lunch box and utensils and in hanging and folding one's uniform. Each step has a single prescribed way it must be completed, and observing that form is central to acquiring proper habits of daily life.

PREPARING TO LEAVE

After stowing their lunch gear and brushing their teeth, children play for thirty to forty-five minutes. At about 1:15 P.M. another cleanup campaign is begun. The teacher sweeps the remnants of lunch from the floor as the children move the chairs into a line and stack the tables against the walls. They then change from their play uniforms into their traveling uniforms. The teacher moves about the room, encouraging children who have difficulty dressing, and buttoning top buttons if necessary. When properly attired in smock, hat, and shoulder bag, each child sits down in his assigned seat. By this time it is usually 1:45 P.M.

After all children have taken their seats, the teacher engages them for five to ten minutes in a teacher-focused, content-oriented group activity, ranging from telling stories from picture cards (*kamishibai*) to playing clapping and listening games or learning a new song. The atmosphere is much more relaxed than during morning announcements. Children who spontaneously call out remarks are usually answered by the teacher, and they sit in a relaxed posture.

Following the group activity, children remove their attendance books from their shoulder bags and sit holding them in their hands. One by one, the teacher calls the name of each child according to the order on the roster. On hearing his name, each child answers *hai* (yes) and walks to the front of the room to receive a small sticker to put over the appropriate space in the calendar in his attendance book. As he returns to his seat, the next child's name is called.

After all students have received their stickers, the teacher again begins at the top of the list, calling each child to the front to receive the parent-teacher message book and any mimeographed notices she may have to send home to the mothers. These procedures require almost fifteen minutes. This time-consuming ritual, which occurred in every preschool visited, is accompanied by a high level of noise and general restlessness. Teachers, however, remain cheerful and unconcerned. When asked about the goal of the activity, teachers justified it vaguely, saying that children were "happy to have their name called" or "liked getting attendance stickers."

The Ministry of Education cites as one of its objectives for use of language in daily life "to answer *hai* when one's name is called." This important classroom skill is also considered a sign of good breeding when exhibited in everyday life. Besides training children in polite response, another implicit objective is to reward and encourage good attendance habits. Great stress is placed on attendance in Japanese schools, and children who have a perfect or nearly perfect attendance record receive prizes at the commence-ment ceremony. The attendance book provides a graphic record of the child's attendance pattern that is easy for him to read. Adding a colorful sticker each day is an enjoyable way of reinforcing good attendance.

The practice of having the entire class wait while each child ap-proaches the teacher for a brief moment of individual attention and positive reinforcement is a common style of traditional Japanese classroom management. It is still frequently observed in settings ranging from calligraphy lessons to elementary-school classes. Teachers are not troubled by the noise and general restlessness of the class, and sooner or later the children learn to relax and enjoy themselves during this period.

DEPARTURE

After passing out the parent-teacher message books, the teacher briefly reviews any important events that have occurred during the day and previews the next day's activities. She then moves to the piano and plays the introduction to the goodbye song. This is the signal for the children to sit up straight, put their hands on their knees, and sing:

> Goodbye, goodbye,
> Today was another day full of fun.
> Goodbye, goodbye,
> I'll see all my friends again tomorrow.

After reciting in unison, "Goodbye, Teacher, goodbye, everyone," the children pick up their chairs and stack them by the wall. They then cluster around the shoe shelf, changing into outdoor shoes. After changing shoes, they run across the playground to their wait-ing mothers.

Dismissal time in Japanese preschools is flexible, ranging from 1:50 to 2:10 P.M., depending on the day's activities and the speed with which the class performs the departure routine. In extreme cases dismissal may be even later. Mothers are instructed to wait outside the fence beginning at 1:50. They stand chatting with one another until the children come out of the classroom.

Mountain City Preschool is typical in that on Saturday children are dismissed at 11:30 A.M. and return home with their mothers for lunch. Most preschools regularly dismiss children before lunch on one or two days of the six-day preschool week (Monbushō 1986, 31).

Teachers make an effort to bow or shake hands and to say *sayōnara* to each of the children as they exit the classroom. They exchange brief greetings or have a short discussion with mothers who approach them, but otherwise they remain near the building. Teachers linger by the doorway, chatting with children whose mothers may be late.

Once all the children have left, the teachers return to their classrooms to clean and sweep them and restore them to order. Afterward they also clean the common areas of the school. Approximately forty-five minutes after the children have left, at 3:00 P.M., they gather for tea in the teachers' room.

At tea the teachers laugh and chat, sometimes recounting incidents that took place during the day. Rarely do they speak in a frustrated or irritated manner about the day's occurrences. Even fights and incidents of misbehavior are recounted warmly and humorously. Following tea, the teachers prepare for upcoming projects or activities, make scenery for the cultural-activities festival, or write monthly newsletters. They usually leave the preschool well before dark, the last teacher locking the door at around 5:00 P.M.

In this chapter we have seen how the rituals and routines of the Japanese preschool day constitute an unwritten curriculum for socializing children in the fundamental habits and attitudes of group life. Comparing our knowledge of Japanese children's life at home and the expectations of the preschool, we see that the difference between the two environments is extreme. Next we will examine the process by which new students learn the routines and practices of preschool life.

PART 3

ENTERING PRESCHOOL

8

Pre-Entrance Events and Ceremonies

For Japanese families, formal preparations for entering preschool begin five or six months before the first day of school. During this period there are a number of scheduled visits by incoming students and their mothers to their chosen school. The long lead time interspersed with trips to the school forms an important transition period. During these months teachers, parents, and children can make unhurried preparation for starting school. Children begin to look forward to becoming a "big" preschooler, and the children and their mothers gain some glimpses of preschool life.

REGISTRATION

The Japanese school year begins in April. Mothers usually begin their informal inquiries concerning the various preschools in the neighborhood during the previous summer. Most preschools require that applications be completed in November for children who wish to begin school the following spring. This six-month preregistration period is typical of the advance planning considered appropriate to making important decisions in Japan. Preschools that have difficulty meeting their desired enrollment quotas may accept applications through December and January. By February it is usually difficult to find a preschool willing to accept a late application.

To register, the mother, usually accompanied by the child, calls briefly at the chosen preschool in November to complete the registration form. If the registration period produces more applicants than there are openings, names are usually drawn from a hat. In Tokyo and other large metropolitan areas a very small number of preschools attached to elite private schools use entrance examinations and selective interviewing. Nationwide, however, these preschools are rare.

INTERVIEW

Following registration, the next occasion on which mother and child formally visit the preschool is for an interview, usually held in December. At that time the mother and child have a chance to meet one or two of the teachers and the director. Teachers usually have not been notified which class they will have in the coming year, so children are not introduced to their future teachers.

During the interview the director and teachers get a sense of the child's personality and family situation, and mothers have an opportunity to call attention to particular characteristics of their child's behavior and personality. The mother completes an information form about the family and typically receives a mimeographed set of instructions on materials to be prepared and childrearing suggestions to ease the transition to preschool. The child is also measured so that properly fitting school uniforms and equipment can be ordered.

The interview itself is normally quite short, lasting about five minutes. Many children are too shy to respond to the teacher, and the information exchanged between mother and teacher is apparently cursory. Nevertheless, in Japanese cultural terms the interview marks the beginning of a formal relationship: it is the first opportunity for the mother, the child, and a representative of the school to *kao o awaseru* (face each other) and acknowledge their new roles and coming affiliation.

The information gained in the interview and entered on the family information sheet is used to assign children to classes. If there is more than one class for each age group, teachers endeavor to balance the classes by gender, birthdate, parental occupation, and the child's personality. Teachers expect difficulty in accurately judging a child's personality in the interview because many traits are at first obscured by shyness. The primary objective is to identify children with special disabilities or obvious problems and distribute them evenly among classes.

The following is a transcript of a typical interview. Although this interview took place at Children's Garden, another preschool in the Mountain City area, the content, the child's reaction, and the exchange between mother and teacher were very similar to those in interviews observed at Mountain City Preschool and Tokyo Preschool.

The teacher moves to the corner of the classroom where a mother and her three-year-old daughter sit at a table awaiting their turn to be interviewed:

1. Teacher: Hello.

2. Mother: Hello. *[To child.]* Say hello. *[Girl hides her face against mother.]*

3. Teacher: Are you a sleepyhead? Tell me your name. Little miss, who are you?

   [A teasing comment on inappropriate behavior.]

4. Mother: Come on. What's your name?

5. Teacher: Yes, please tell me your name. *[Using play voice and stuffed toy snake.]* Little miss, who are you? What's your name? *[Whispers.]* Please tell Mr. Snake. *[Regular voice.]* You won't? You won't. Then shall I ask your mommy? Huh?

6. Mother: Yes. She should say, "My name is Kobayashi Yuka."

7. Teacher: Yuka?

8. Child: *[Face averted, whining.]* Ouch! Ouch! *[Rubs leg.]*

9. Teacher: *[Laughs.]* Are you Mrs. Kobayashi?

   [Mother and teacher briefly remove the pressure on Yuka by speaking to each other.]

10. Mother: Yes.

11. Teacher: *[Speaking to Yuka through mother.]* So Yuka's papa has a sushi shop?

12. Mother: *[Indirectly to teacher through child.]* Tell Teacher yes. With Grandma and Grandpa.

13. Teacher: So Grandma and Grandpa have a sushi shop, do they? Huh, Yuka? How old are you? *[Yuka hides face in mother's lap.]* Oh, oh! She's fallen asleep again!

    [Teasing comment on inappropriate behavior.]

14. Mother: How old are you? Huh? How old?

15. Teacher: How old? Three? Huh,
    Yuka-chan? *[Laughs.]* What do
    you think this is? *[Holds up snake.]*
    Munch, munch, munch. *[Makes
    snake pretend to eat Yuka's neck.]*
    What do you think this is?

16. Mother: *[Mildly.]* Come on. What
    are you hiding for? Look at the
    teacher. Right now. Be nice. Stop
    it. What is that the teacher's
    holding?

17. Teacher: *[Laughs.]* Mr. Snake's
    going away, look. He's going to
    hide in here. Look, he's all gone
    now.

    *["Your friends are
    going away" is a com-
    mon technique of coax-
    ing children who
    refuse to participate.]*

18. Mother: Sit up properly.

19. Teacher: Please talk to the snake.
    Look. Are you terribly sleepy?
    [Play voice.] Good morning, it's
    time to wake up! *[Laughs.]*

    *[Teasing comment on
    inappropriate
    behavior.]*

20. Mother: Yuka, you have to sit up
    nicely. *[Attempts to push head up.]*

21. Teacher: Shall I show you how to
    sit up properly? *[Approaches.]*

    *[Clear signaling of in-
    appropriate behavior.]*

22. Child: No! No! Don't! No!

23. Teacher: Yuka.

24. Mother: You mustn't act like this.

25. Child: *[Wailing.]* No! *[Gets up from
    chair and runs behind mother to bury
    her face in mother's back.]*

26. *[Mother and teacher laugh.]*

27. Child: No! Go away!

28. *[Mother and teacher laugh.]*

29. Teacher: Can she use the
    bathroom by herself?

    *[Mother and teacher
    redirect the conversa-
    tion to each other.]*

30. Mother: Yes, when she feels like
    it, she can do it by herself, but
    right now because she has a new
    baby brother, she's showing *amae*
    and I have to be right there and
    help her with everything.

    *[Mother accepts toilet-
    ing* amae *as a demand
    for her attention.]*

31. Teacher: But at least she can do it at times?

32. Mother: She's been known to do it alone sometimes. She's used to removing all her lower clothing.

33. Teacher: Is the toilet at home Western-style?

34. Mother: We have one of each. She can use both, but someone has to hold her over the Japanese-style one.

[Yuka clearly will require help in using the Japanese-style toilets at preschool, but teacher does not encourage mother to increase Yuka's self-sufficiency.]

35. Teacher: I see. Thank you very much.

36. Child: Mama, I want to go home.

37. Teacher: Yes, it's time to go. *[All stand.]* Well, I'll see you on school visitation day. Goodbye. Can you say goodbye to Teacher?

38. Mother: Say goodbye.

39. Yuka: *[Hides face in mother's skirt.]*

40. *[Mother and teacher laugh.]*

41. Teacher: Here is a sheet explaining what you'll need to prepare. The preschool will present everyone with their shoulder bags. That's all. Goodbye.

42. Mother: We request your kind consideration [*yoroshiku onegai shimasu*]. Goodbye. *[To Yuka.]* Can't you say goodbye? Say goodbye.

[A polite formula used in making requests.]

43. Yuka: No.

44. Mother: *[Smiling.]* Goodbye.

45. Teacher: Goodbye.

Yuka's inability to speak to the teacher and her attempts to hide her face are termed *tereru* (shyness), an initial shrinking on social contact common among Japanese children. It is usually met with laughter and teasing comments. Although some degree of timidity in dealings with strangers is considered charming, Japanese parents, teachers, and childrearing advisers all agree that being able to greet others in a clearly enunciated, cheerful manner is a skill that should be inculcated early in children. It is one of the most commonly listed behaviors for mothers to encourage their children to master before they enter preschool. In practice, however, children's difficulty in doing this is not taken as a serious problem. Teachers actually regard the development of this social skill as something likely to require several years.

The considerable pressure focused on Yuka to get her to respond is typical of mild methods of correcting behavior used by Japanese preschool teachers. The teacher's teasing remarks repeatedly approach a climax, at which both mother and teacher briefly relieve the pressure and change the subject by laughing (8–9, 15, 16–17, 25–26). The comments leading up to the climax signal that the child's behavior is inappropriate ("Are you a sleepyhead?" [3]; "Shall I show you how to sit up properly?" [21]; "Good morning, it's time to wake up!" [19]). The laughter signals that the child's response to these comments is also inappropriate and, although childishly charming, is somewhat ridiculous.

At the age of three or four, most children are not yet sophisticated enough to be sensitive to this technique and therefore persist unconcerned. By age five or six, however, children immediately become embarrassed at such jesting comments and laughter and either immediately exhibit appropriate behavior or shrink and blush in embarrassment. In children as young as Yuka this technique rarely produces an immediate change in behavior.

The mimeographed sheet sent home with the mother at the time of the interview usually lists those articles of clothing and pieces of equipment to be prepared before the opening ceremony and the first day of school. It also describes the preschool's expectations regarding what the child should be able to do when he enters preschool. The following message from a public preschool in Tokyo is typical (italics as in original):

Before Your Child Enters Preschool

This April, your child, who has developed rapidly in the warm hothouse of the family, will for the first time be propelled into the outside world. He will enter preschool, which means becoming one member of a group-based society of children his own age. Family members, particularly the mother, feel their hearts swell with expectation yet have countless worries about their child—can he manage to follow along?

We suggest that each mother and child concentrate on the following goals until April:

1. Can your child eat by himself?
2. Can he tell the difference between his own and others' things?
3. Can he tell people if his stomach hurts?
4. Can he walk single file on the right-hand side of the street?
5. Can he greet others politely?
6. Can he button his own clothing? *Can he take his clothing on and off by himself?*
7. Can he use the bathroom when he needs to?
8. *Can he have a bowel movement unassisted?*
9. Can he blow his own nose?
10. *Does he understand what kinds of places are dangerous, and can he avoid them?*

These goals become meaningless if the mother becomes hurried or impatient. The mother's nervous feelings will be communicated to the child, who will feel anxious about preschool life. We hope that you will patiently and gradually build one day at a time.

The first step in preschool life is to learn to play with one's friends and the teacher. *Everything starts from play.* If your child is able to play, you need have no concern.

Just as your child is taking a big first step in entering preschool, you are taking a big first step in becoming the mother of a preschool child. Even if this is your second or third child, this particular child is taking his first step on a long journey, so please refresh your heart as you set out with him.

We see reiterated here several themes that were examined in depth in previous chapters. Entering preschool is described as a transition from the warmly nurturant environment of the family to the less sympathetic environment of group life. The mother is encouraged to undertake her own new role seriously, identifying herself as a new student along with her child. Play is the primary means by which the child's interest in and affiliation with preschool life is secured, and the enthusiasm arising from play is slowly shaped to include other ends.

In practice, the ten self-sufficiency goals the handout lists are regarded more as ideals than actual prerequisites for entering preschool. As we have already seen, many children do not meet even half of these goals at the time they enter preschool. Nonetheless, parents and teachers take a remarkably long view. For example, Yuka's interview reveals that she was largely unable to use the toilet unassisted, too shy to speak when spoken to by strangers, and frightened at the teacher's approach. However, her apparent lack of readiness for preschool was not viewed as serious enough for the teacher to comment on during the interview or for the teacher to recommend special preparatory procedures. In Japan it is implicitly understood that there will often be considerable discrepancy between official and actual expectations.

SCHOOL VISITATION DAY

Most preschools hold a school visitation day for new mothers and students in March, called "entering preschool for a single day" (*ichi nichi nyūen*). At this event the continuing students host the incoming students and their mothers. Activities typically center around presentations and speeches rather than giving children a chance to experience a normal day of preschool life. The purpose of school visitation day is to encourage a feeling of anticipation and reassurance in the incoming students and their mothers.

School visitation day at Mountain City Preschool was held in early March, just a month before the beginning of school. The incoming students and their mothers arrived at the school at 10:30 A.M. and returned home after an hour-long ceremony, which was held in the middle of a regular five-hour school day for the other children.

During the morning play period, teachers held an informal run-through of the operetta from the previous month's cultural-activities festival, which the older children had decided to present. A few students helped another teacher set up chairs in the activity room for the incoming students and their mothers. The class of three-year-olds temporarily moved their belongings into the four-year-olds' room to provide a place for the newcomers and their mothers to gather.

As the new students and their mothers began to arrive in the schoolyard, the continuing students ran to the windows and out onto the porch to look. They jumped up and down in excitement, remarking loudly, "Cute!" "So little!" and "Teeny-tiny!" The new mothers and children changed their shoes and entered the three-year-olds' room. Once they were inside, the director welcomed each mother and child politely, pinning a tulip-shaped construction-paper name tag on the child, and handing the mother an envelope (for enclosing money to purchase uniforms and supplies) and a program detailing the day's order of ceremonies.

Some of the new children sat in the chairs provided; others moved about exploring the room. Still others stood with their mothers along the walls while the women talked politely with each other. Older students ran in and out of the room to look, ineffectively shooed away from time to time by the director. One new boy, unnerved by the situation, kept his face buried in his mother's skirts, crying loudly. His mother, who carried a large baby strapped to her back, alternately ignored her crying son and asked what was wrong. Between sobs his only answer was *iya da*, a childishly petulant combination of "no" and "I don't like this." As his crying continued without abating, the mother bent down, placed her hands on his shoulders, and said quietly but intensely, "With all your friends here this is embarrassing. Tell me *what* you don't like. Tell me." The child continued to cry, mumbling unintelligibly. "You'll have to speak louder. If you can't tell me what is *iya da*, cut it out." She then stood up and ignored him, and the child kept crying.

A minute to two later the director came over to them, asking, "My goodness, what's the matter?" The mother knelt down to the child's level and told him, "You must say 'hello' nicely to the teacher. Tell her what is *iya da*." The child tried to bury his head against his mother. The director laughed, saying, "What is *iya da*? Look, here are lots of friends to play with." She smiled, then turned to all the mothers: "We are ready to begin." The mother of the crying child once more stood up and ignored him, and he continued to sob, burying his head in her skirts.

The director moved to the front of the room and called the roll. Each child—or, if he was too shy, his mother—responded *hai* (yes). The teacher then made some brief administrative remarks to the mothers concerning the money envelope. She then asked the mothers to form a line with their children as she again called each child's name in order from the roster.

At 10:40 the line of mothers and children filed into the activity room, where the older classes stood in rows, clapping and singing a welcoming song. The new children sat in a double row of child-sized chairs, and the mothers sat in larger chairs behind them. Continuing students sat in rows on the floor.

Speaking informally, the director announced that the welcoming ceremony had begun and called for another round of applause for all of "our cute new friends." After encouraging everyone to "have a lot of fun today," she introduced the principal, who gave a short speech, abridged here:

> Good morning. Today is your child's first day at preschool. Suddenly his solitary world at home has opened into a big new world. This is his first step into society. He is slowly growing up.
>
> The preschool years are important ones in your child's development. Many people think that three-year-olds can't learn much. That is not true. It is a very important time when the brain is growing rapidly.
>
> Attending preschool is important. In three years, when your child graduates, he will have matured more than you can now imagine. He will make friends, with whom he will fight and laugh. He will learn to become a member of a group.
>
> Mountain City Preschool's goals are to develop the body, heart, and mind. The most important thing we hope our students will learn is respect and appreciation for parents, teachers, and God. We look forward to having your child at our preschool. Thank you.

During the principal's speech all of the children became extremely restless. Four or five new and continuing students had left their places, running back and forth across the room in front of the speaker. Two boys in the three-year-olds' class had a noisy tussle, calling each other loudly and repeatedly *bakayarō*, an obscenity meaning idiot. Teachers and parents ignored the tussle and the distractions.

The director now took the floor, remarking that it was nice some children had already begun to make friends. She led the entire group in singing a well-known children's song, in which many of the incoming children joined. She then asked the new children to listen carefully and learn as their older friends sang the school song, and she asked the mothers to teach the song to their children at home.

Then the class of five-year-olds presented a twenty-minute operetta, *The Treasure at the Bottom of the Lake*, which they had presented the previous month at the school cultural festival. Although most of the children watched the presentation with interest, by the end of the performance some of the new students had again left their chairs and were running about. Teachers and mothers ignored them.

The director then stood up, remarking with a polite apology that the performance had been long. She asked the new mothers to look forward to the day when their child would be in the five-year-olds' class and they would also be capable of staging such a performance. Then she announced that each child had a gift to give the new students. The three-year-olds had made construction-paper crowns with dog faces on them, and the four- and five-year-olds had made paper necklaces. The teachers then called the continuing students one at a time to come forward to reclaim their artwork. After four or five minutes each child was in possession of the gift he had made for the incoming students.

Then the entire group sang a song about dogs, relating to the dog-faced paper crowns the new students were to receive. Next, the director asked the three-year-olds to put their hats on the new children and tell each of them, "Please come to preschool in good health." Then the four-year-olds and finally the five-year-olds put their handmade gifts on the new students.

After the children returned to their seats, the director made a brief speech to the mothers:

> All of us at preschool are looking forward to the arrival of the new little ones. Please help your child feel that preschool will be an enjoyable place. The next time you come will be for the opening ceremony on April 10. Don't be late. Bring your child dressed in his uniform, with a handkerchief and a packet of tissues in his pocket. From then on, you should send him so prepared every day. Before the first day of school, be sure to label all of the child's equipment and clothing. That includes handkerchiefs, socks, and underwear.
>
> April 11 will be the first regular preschool day. The classes of three- and four-year-olds will be in session from 8:40 to 10:00 A.M. That will be the first day your child will have to leave your side. Each child reacts differently to leaving his mother. Some children cry. If you say, "It's okay. You'll be alright," it won't be too hard for your child. Don't say, "Don't cry, don't cry." Your child should feel that he can let his feelings show. Whatever you say, don't let your *own* bittersweet feelings show on your face. Come, drop off your child, and leave. If mothers remain within eyesight, the children won't settle down. When your return to pick your child up, remain outside the fence.
>
> From the preschool's point of view, our goals for these first days

are for the child to be able to remain physically at preschool and to be able to use the toilet if he needs to. Some children try to leave the grounds and run back home. Others are so nervous that they retain their natural functions and wet their pants as soon as they leave the preschool. Your child probably won't be able to tell you what he did during these first days because he will be so engrossed in the new-ness of everything that he won't remember.

Until children enter preschool, their experience has been con-fined to mother and at most three or four other children. Now they will be in a new environment with sixty other children their own age. We will keep an eye on how they adjust and notify you through the parent-teacher message book.

Please change your child's sleep schedule well in advance so that he wakes up early each morning and goes to bed early each evening. If you have to drag him out of bed in the morning to come to pre-school, he won't be in a good mood. Change his schedule so that he arrives at preschool relaxed and well-prepared for the day.

Many of you will be worried that your child can't use the toilet alone. If he can't, don't impatiently try to teach him all at once. En-courage him to tell the teacher that he needs to go to the bathroom. It's important that your child be able to express his needs and feelings.

Particularly if this is your first child, you may be nervous and worried about various things. Please ask if you have any questions.

It is good to see that many children have already begun to make friends. The next time you come to the preschool will be for the opening ceremony on April 10. Don't be late. Please leave the house with a smile on your face and a cheerful feeling in your heart. Thank you very much.

During the speech both old and new students had become ex-tremely restless, and thirteen children were out of their seats and moving about the room. The obscenities accompanying another tussle between two four-year-old boys—*bakayarō* and *aho* (fool)—had started a wave of obscenity calling from various parts of the room. As parents and teachers listened to the director's speech apparently undisturbed, children tried to outdo one another in demonstrating their knowledge of illicit words. One particularly daring five-year-old topped the list with *unko* (feces) and *chinpoko* (penis). Completely ignored by teachers and parents, the contest died down as the audience rose to leave. The director's remark "It is good to see that many children have already begun to make friends" was a veiled reference to the general commotion.

After the end of the ceremony was announced, there was a round of polite applause, and the mothers returned to the three-year-olds' room to pick up their children's new uniforms and equipment and to hand in their money envelopes. They then dressed the children in coats and scarves and, bowing goodbye to the director, left for home. The entire event had taken exactly one hour.

School visitation day represents the second step in gradually acclimatizing children to the preschool environment. The first chance to see the preschool is during the interview, when children enter the building while other students are not present and interact briefly with the teachers. On school visitation day children have a chance to glimpse the life of the preschool and the activities of other children while school is in session. They are allowed to be passive observers, watching the activities of the older children from the safety of their mother's side.

A period of "learning through watching" (*minarai kikan*), that is, of requiring prospective students to sit on the sidelines and watch the activities of the older students, is a traditional feature of Japanese learning situations (Peak 1986). Although longer than a single day, its form and content are in many ways similar to those of school visitation day. Prospective classmates watch passively as uniformed older students go about their activities; attention is directed toward the older students rather than the teacher. New students are expected to absorb rituals and symbols of group membership, such as singing the school song, through observation. In the process of watching, a strong desire to join the group arises, and children develop an understanding of their future role.

Once the child desires to join the group, receiving recognition from older students is an important motivating force. Symbolically, the dog crowns and paper necklaces are more than trifling gifts. Their individualized bestowal and the formula "Please come to preschool in good health" represent an invitation from the older children to the prospective members to join the group. Such welcoming gestures, together with the presentation of regulation equipment and uniforms, are a common first step in joining Japanese organizations of all types.

On school visitation day every effort is made to make the new children's first encounter with the preschool environment as positive as possible. Virtually nothing was requested or expected of the children, and they were allowed to watch as they liked and to do as they pleased. Even older children were not disciplined or corrected in the presence of the new students. As the director remarked to the mothers, the goal of the day is to allow children to see the preschool as an enjoyable place. Once the child has psychologically committed himself to membership, there will be sufficient time after he has formally joined the group to modify his behavior. This relaxed atmosphere contrasts greatly with the much higher expectations of children's behavior once they have actually become a part of the group at the opening ceremony.

Mothers and teachers have different views on the acceptability of crying under the stress of a new situation. The mother of the boy who cried before the ceremony made several earnest attempts to get her son to stop, telling him that his loud sobs were embarrassing. In interviews many mothers reported worrying that their children would cry when left at preschool. Although this worry could have stemmed from concern that their child would be upset or lonely, the mothers' specific mention of crying was probably significant. The director, however, instructed mothers not to tell their children "Don't cry," describing crying as a legitimate way for children to let their feelings show.

Japanese mothers tend to differ from teachers as regards the acceptability of letting inappropriate feelings show. Mothers, well socialized themselves, identify with their children in social situations and consistently encourage them to restrain their inappropriate feelings rather than expose themselves to embarrassment. The mothers quoted in chapter 1 clearly expected children to "pull their wings in" and be on their best behavior at preschool.

Teachers also expect that children who have been fully socialized in group behavior will be able to hold back inappropriate feelings, although they understand that not all children will be able to do so initially. There are two ways of understanding teachers' frequent insistence that children should frankly express even negative feelings. First, the teacher, who is an outsider entrusted with another's child, is at pains to reassure the mother that the child's inappropriate behavior is not offensive to her. The director's statement "Your child should feel that he can let his feelings show" is a variety of the standard polite invitation to suspend commonly accepted rules of behavior that is a form of etiquette between strangers in a Japanese social situation. Such an invitation, however, is never accepted by a fully socialized member of society. Second, teachers realize that it is ultimately ineffective to attempt to enforce behavioral expectations beyond the child's actual level of social understanding. Demands for appropriate behavior are implemented gradually and individually, each child being dealt with at his own level.

9

Opening Ceremony

Matriculation at schools of all types in Japan is marked by a formal entrance ceremony. Advancement to the next level of schooling is an occasion for congratulations and gifts from friends and family members. Because children's social identity is largely defined by the level of school they attend, becoming a preschooler, an elementary-school student, or a high-school student is an important transition in Japanese children's lives.

The entrance ceremony also signals the beginning of the child's formal status as a student at a particular school and his acceptance as a member of that student community. Even for three- and four-year-olds, the new uniform, new people, new role, and new environment combine with the formality of the ceremony to leave a strong impression. Despite their limited social experience, they seem to realize that they have assumed a new, more mature identity and that new behavior will be expected of them.

On the day of the opening ceremony at Mountain City Preschool, the teachers arrived earlier than usual, dressed in freshly laundered uniforms. They carefully swept and raked the entire building and grounds. Then they put up the welcoming decorations, which consisted of a large banner over the school gate announcing "Mountain City Preschool—Fifty-first Entrance Ceremony" and garlands of construction-paper flowers over the doors of the three- and four-year-olds' classrooms. Everything was ready by the time the director, principal, and president of the PTA arrived. Continuing students came to school a little earlier than usual so that they would be at the preschool when the new children arrived.

Thirty minutes before the ceremony was scheduled to begin, new students and their mothers started to arrive. Mothers were dressed in their best clothes, with hair freshly coiffed and makeup carefully applied. Children wore their brand-new uniforms self-consciously.

As the new students and their mothers entered the preschool grounds, they were met at the gate by the director and the teacher of the five-year-olds' class. Polite greetings were exchanged, and the teacher selected the child's permanent plastic name tag from a table in front of her and pinned it on his uniform.

Mothers and children then crossed the school yard to the door of the classroom. Here the children's new classroom teacher was waiting to meet them, and another set of formal greetings was exchanged. Each mother took out her child's brand-new pair of indoor shoes and put them on him, leaving his outdoor shoes on the shoe shelf.

Inside the classroom the teacher showed each child his own hook and pointed out his identifying sticker and his name. The mother then helped the child remove and hang up his hat. The teacher spoke warmly to each child, remarking to several how handsome they looked in their new uniforms. Children and mothers then stood waiting in the classroom.

Ten minutes before the ceremony was to begin, all of the new students and their mothers had assembled in the three-year-olds' classroom, and continuing students were seated in place in the room in which the ceremony was to be held. The director invited the mothers to take their seats for the ceremony, leaving the new students behind with their teacher.

As soon as the mothers had left the room, the boy who had cried on school visitation day asked loudly and anxiously of no one in particular, "Mama? Where's my Mama? Where did my Mama go?" The teacher replied "Just like last time, the big boys and girls are going to do something nice for us. Your Mama? I wonder where she went. She's coming right back." The child continued to look about anxiously but did not cry.

The teacher then lined the children up by telling them to make a train, each child with his hands on the shoulders of the child in front of him. She selected the most distractible and restless boy as the line leader. With that child's hands on her hips, making train-like sounds, she towed the line to the corridor outside the room in which the ceremony was to be held. Then she stopped to wait for the signal to enter.

A comical five minutes ensued, as first one and then another child tired of standing in position and began to wander off. The teacher called after them in a friendly manner, sometimes going over to take a child's hand and lead him back into the line: "If the driver wanders off, our train is going to be in trouble"; "Oh, oh, a car has escaped. Please wait here"; "When we're ready to start, I'll say, 'Here we go.' Until then make your body soft and relaxed and take a little rest"; "Wait, wait, just a little longer. Oh, oh, there goes the driver again. Please hold him firmly so our train doesn't wreck."

At last the signal came for the train to move off, and the line of new students entered the room to a rousing march played on the piano and loud applause from the older students and the mothers. After the new children filed into their places and were seated, the director made the following welcoming remarks:

> Good morning. *[All respond in chorus, "good morning."]* What a cheerful and enthusiastic response! Today is the day we have all been waiting and waiting for—the day of the entrance ceremony. Beginning today you are a student at Mountain City Preschool. Everyone has a bright and shiny face.
>
> For a little while we will sing some songs and listen while some people talk. Let's close our mouths "um," put our hands on our knees, straighten our backs, show a little perseverance, and listen hard. Can you do it? *[All respond in chorus, "Yes."]* That's good.
>
> Then the Fifty-first Opening Ceremony of Mountain City Preschool will now begin. I request your kind consideration.
>
> First in the order of ceremonies is the school song. Every morning we sing this song when we say hello to each other. Each of you has two hands. Show them to me. *[She holds up both hands, fluttering them above her head. All the children imitate.]* What clean and pretty hands. Now, gently, gently, put them together and put them quietly in front of your chest. All older students stand up quietly. That's good. Now can our new friends stand up too? That's fine. Now stretch your backs nice and straight. How wonderful you all look! How skillful you are! Now, just like this, let's sing the school song quietly and nicely. Mothers please fold your hands and sing with us. Piano, please . . . *[Following the piano introduction, all sing the school song.]*
>
> Thank you very much. Now you can all sit down. Next, the most important person in the school, the principal, will speak to us. Put your hands on your knees. Stretch your back up nice and straight. Fix your eyes on the principal's face. Now, let's listen to what he will tell us. Principal, please be kind enough to speak to us.

Here the principal took the floor:

> Good morning, everyone. From today you are all students at Mountain City Preschool. What big boys and girls you have become.

Please, everyone in the blue class and the yellow class [four- and five-year-olds] take good care of our new friends in the pink class [three-year-olds]. Be nice to them, teach them songs, and run and play with them. You are the big brothers and sisters at Mountain City Preschool now, so please do whatever you can to help the pink class. Everyone please come to preschool enthusiastically each day and play together happily with your friends. That is all. Thank you very much.

During the principal's brief speech the level of background noise climbed considerably. Children called out "Stop it," "Be quiet," and "You're too noisy." A tussle broke out between two continuing four-year-olds, and a nearby girl cautioned loudly, "Stop fighting." A teacher moved to stand near the children and looked sternly at them, and they calmed down.

The director again spoke: "Thank you very much, Principal. Next the continuing students have some words of welcome for our new friends. Blue and yellow classes please stand up." The four- and five-year-olds stood up and, led by a teacher, recited in unison, "Hello. We are happy you have come to be our new friends at Mountain City Preschool. We have a swing set and a slide. Let's play together." They then sang a song that they had chosen for the new students.

Next, the assistant principal took the floor to introduce each of the teachers and to announce which class they had been assigned to teach. He then requested each of the new students to stand one at a time and give their name. Almost all of the children were able to say their name clearly. The several who were too shy had their name announced by the teacher.

The director then continued:

We begin the fifty-first year of the preschool's existence with a total of sixty children, fourteen in the pink class and seventeen in the yellow class. In the blue class, who are the older brothers and sisters and know everything here at the preschool, there are twenty-nine students. This concludes the introductions.

Next we will have a few brief words from the president of the PTA. First, let's check. Where are your hands? Where should they be when you are listening? [*All respond in chorus, "On your knees."*] What about your back? Make it straight and tall. Which way is your face pointing? Point it toward the person who is speaking. Now we are ready to hear from the PTA president.

The PTA president gave the following speech:

Congratulations on your preschool matriculation. From now on, you must listen nicely to what the teachers say. Make lots and lots of friends and play with them happily. I'm sure that sometimes there will be fights, but you will make up again soon.

A word to the mothers, particularly those whose first child is entering preschool. Right now your hearts are probably brimming with anticipation and worries. The best characteristic of this preschool is that it allows the children to play freely. I'm sure that many of you have your own opinions about this, but please leave it in the teachers' hands.

From today, the mothers must work together, just as the children must work together, to create a happy atmosphere at the preschool. There will be various PTA activities that will require your cooperation. We request your active assistance throughout the year. Thank you.

The director again took the floor:

Things will become more and more exciting tomorrow. Your child should arrive at school tomorrow and every day between eight-forty and nine in the morning. Please don't be late. Some classes are still missing members even by nine o'clock. At nine, classes enter their rooms for morning greetings. If your child isn't present at morning greetings, his entire day will not go well. I ask you not to be late.

As the PTA president said, I understand that new mothers will have many worries. However, from the preschool's side, we will do everything we can to protect your child's safety. Don't worry if your child sometimes cries a bit at preschool. Learning to overcome difficulties makes children's hearts strong.

Every year for the past fifty years, rows of mothers just like you, with feelings in their hearts just like yours, have sat in this room and sent their children off to preschool. Please talk to the mothers of older children, ask their advice, and become friendly with them. They will help you as you reflect on your own child's experience. From the preschool's side, we request your kind consideration and cooperation through the years.

By this time children were shifting in their chairs, which were clattering against the floor, and the director's voice had become almost inaudible. She observed:

Just as the ceremony is becoming interesting and enjoyable, the allotted time unfortunately is drawing to a close. At this point let us calm our hearts and bring the ceremony to a close. Blue, yellow, and pink classes, let us fold our hands. With a calm and quiet feeling let us listen to the piano before we finish. [*The pianist plays a fifteen-second wordless song used daily after the goodbye song.]* This concludes the Fifty-first Opening Ceremony. Thank you very much.

The new members of the pink and yellow classes immediately filed out of the room to the applause of their mothers and the five-year-olds. They returned to their classrooms, where they were soon joined by their mothers. As soon as all of the new mothers and children had arrived in the classroom, the teacher of the three-year-old class made the following speech to her students' mothers:

My name is Suzuki Michiko, and I will be the regular teacher of the pink class. Throughout the coming year I will try to do my best, along with all the members of the class.

This is the first time these children have been in a group environment. Today things were pretty boisterous. There may be some children who will find it hard to adjust. The beginning will be a little difficult for everyone—for you mothers and especially for the children. Because it is the first time the children have had a group experience, at first it will be difficult for them, and they won't function together well. Gradually they will become accustomed to it. Right now, *everything* is new to them, so all at once I won't say "Do this, stop that, and take care of these things by yourself." Without overdoing it, I'll try to ask this much today and a little bit more tomorrow, never rushing and never stopping. Please do the same at home. The goals of this preschool are "Energy, Cheerfulness, and Harmony." Please try to reinforce these in your family as well.

I would like to have as many opportunities as possible for communication between the preschool and your family. The things we need to notify you about from the preschool's side we will send home with your child as mimeographed sheets. For person-to-person remarks between mother and teacher, we will use the mother-teacher message book. You can tell me things you notice about the child at home, and I will tell you things I notice about him at school. I hope that we will communicate easily with each other throughout the year. I will do my best in caring for your child this year. I request your kind consideration.

Afterward the teacher delivered a ten-minute explanation of various administrative matters—labeling of clothing, arrival and dismissal times, procedures in case of absence, and so on. At the end of her remarks she passed out the regulation supplies the children would use during the year, including crayons, castanets, sketch books, and other items. As each child's name was called from the roster, he came forward to receive the equipment and pass it to his mother. His mother then put it in a bag handmade according to specifications distributed on school visitation day.

After the materials were distributed, everyone went outdoors into the school yard to line up for a formal group photograph. Then the new students and their mothers left for home, and the continuing students waited for their mothers to pick them up.

Mountain City Preschool's opening ceremony was similar in both form and content to the entrance cermonies observed in other preschools and even those of elementary schools. The ceremonial procession of the new children, the formal statement "The ceremony will now begin," the singing of the school song, the introduction of teachers, the announcement of the total number of enrollees, the group recitation of a welcoming statement to the new students, speeches by the principal and the president of the PTA— all these elements recurred in the other opening ceremonies witnessed. Many of the sentiments and remarks were also repeated in each of the ceremonies—references to the bright and shiny faces, to enrollees becoming big boys and girls, to older children helping the younger ones, to mothers' hearts full of worry and anticipation, as well as a formal request for the mothers' cooperation and consideration. These highly similar ceremonies took place in different types of schools and in different parts of the country, but all seem to be based on the same unwritten but universally accepted cultural scenario.

The ceremony reveals several practices central to understanding how children's transition from home to preschool is facilitated. First, as much as possible, reprimanding of misbehavior was avoided in preference for explicit training of appropriate behavior. For example, to begin of each part of the ceremony, children were told exactly how to position their bodies, and teachers directed the students in a standard routine for assuming proper posture. To have the new students, who had never stood in line before, line up to march into the ceremony, the children were told to make a train with hands on shoulders and then to remain that way. Instead of repeatedly reminding children to behave properly after their attention had lapsed, teachers waited until the beginning of the next activity to bring them to attention in preparation for a fresh start. This technique was particularly effective in training young children to come to order while avoiding the negativity associated with continually correcting misbehavior.

Training in proper posture includes training in appropriate feeling or sentiment. Indeed, the Japanese word *taido*, which is often used in this context, refers to both posture and mental attitude. The three-year-olds were told to wait in line "with your body soft and relaxed." For the solemn moment of the closing song, they were instructed, "Fold your hands, put them in front of your chest, and listen with a calm and quiet feeling." This approach to training the proper physical and mental attitude is used often during the first weeks of preschool. It is also common in a wide variety of Japanese educational settings for students of all ages.

The behavior and affect expected of mothers was also subtly but clearly explained. Although the PTA president's acknowledgment that the mothers' hearts were "probably brimming with anticipation and worries" focused on each mother's feeling for her own child, mothers were encouraged to develop some detachment: they were reminded that each was one of thousands of such mothers in the preschool's history, all of whose children had presumably successfully negotiated the experience. Detachment extended to the details of their children's coming experiences at preschool: "Many of you have your own opinions about this, but leave it in the teacher's hands"; "Don't worry if your child cries a bit at preschool. Learning to overcome difficulties makes children's hearts strong."

At the entrance ceremony, speakers clearly specified the appropriate channels for mothers' relationships to the preschool. Full participation in PTA activities was requested. Spur-of-the-moment telephoning and dropping by after hours for informal conferences with the teacher were not mentioned, therefore in Japanese cultural terms they were tacitly discouraged. Just as the children were instructed in the appropriate posture for listening to a speech, their mothers were more subtly guided in the appropriate form of mother-teacher communication. The teacher's wish that she and the mothers "communicate easily" actually implies proper observance of the recommended forms of communication rather than entirely open and honest communication. As we shall see in part 4 on adjustment problems, mother-teacher communication is rarely completely candid.

The mother's interest in and desire to assist her child's education is explicitly channeled into proper fulfillment of maternal roles—involvement in the PTA, careful preparation of the child's belongings, and getting the child to school on time. This participation does not extend to expressing opinions about classroom activities. The president of the PTA, besides requesting that mothers leave the school's activities and curricular emphases in the teachers' hands, also reminded them that a happy preschool atmosphere depends on mothers working together to fulfill their responsibilities, just as children must fulfill theirs.

Children were encouraged to rely on older students, "the older brothers and sisters [who] know everything here at the preschool." The older children were encouraged to help and teach the new students. Similarly, new mothers were encouraged to rely on the more experienced mothers of older children for advice. This hierarchy greatly facilitates the transition into the routine and rituals of preschool life by providing age-appropriate leadership and role models. It also allows older children and more experienced mothers the opportunity to feel pride in being the new cohort's tutors and reinforces their awareness of good behavior and the importance of setting a good example.

Another theme running through the opening ceremony is the recognition that appropriate behavior is a skill that initially is difficult but can eventually be mastered. Anticipating and being psychologically prepared for difficulties removes much of their threat when they arise. For example, the director told the children that they would need perseverance to remain well behaved throughout the ceremony and asked, "Can you do it?" The PTA president acknowledged that children will fight sometimes, "but you will make up again soon." Mothers were expected to have differences of opinion with the teachers, "but please leave it in the teachers' hands." The classroom teacher expected children to have difficulty adjusting to the demands of the group environment but planned to increase her expectations gradually. "Never rushing and never stopping" and realizing that "overcom[ing] difficulties makes children's hearts strong" are important attitudes that shape the techniques of training behavior in early learning environments in Japan.

Taken together, the long registration period, the interview, school visitation day, and the entrance ceremony constitute a key to Japanese children's successful transition to preschool life. They allow new students and their mothers to adjust gradually to the new environment through increasingly extended glimpses of preschool life. Acknowledging that difficulties will arise and will be overcome, the preschool does everything possible to make an initially positive and nonthreatening impression on the new children. Without exception, mothers reported that their children looked forward excitedly to wearing their brand-new uniform and to joining the big boys and girls on the first day of school. Many children had been counting the days until preschool began for several weeks.

The transition period creates in the new students and their mothers a high degree of anticipation and excitement about entering preschool life. It also tries to give them some understanding of their new role and a sense of stretching toward a new, more mature identity. During the first days of school, the teachers' task is to mold this excitement in the direction of appropriate classroom behavior.

10

The First Weeks of School

The beginning of the year in a Japanese preschool is not easy. Until children learn the daily routines of preschool and begin to strive toward self-sufficiency, classrooms are chaotic, and a great deal of time is required to accomplish even simple activities. Tears, tantrums, and refusal to attend school are common. Teachers remain cheerful and optimistic through the confusion, confident that the children will ultimately become accustomed to classroom life.

Teachers reported that the 1984 class of three-year-olds in Mountain City Preschool required slightly more time to negotiate the transition than usual but was not atypical. This may have been due to the large number of boys. Boys are said to have more difficulty adjusting to preschool because at home they are raised to be *wagamama* (expecting to get their own way). For the purpose of this study, it was perhaps fortuitous that the students in the primary field site experienced somewhat more adjustment problems than average, for the situation allowed a more intense and diverse sampling of the types of problems that occur during transition than might otherwise have been observed.

Most of the main characteristics of the first weeks of school at Mountain City Preschool were similar to those observed at Tokyo Preschool. They also corresponded to the reports of the directors of other preschools. Each class, of course, had its own unique personality and atmosphere.

SCHEDULING OF THE FIRST DAYS OF PRESCHOOL

Preschools try to make the first days go as smoothly as possible for the new children. The five-hour school day is shortened to two and a half hours. New students return home early while older students remain for the regular day. Teachers maintain that new students get tired easily and therefore need a shorter day at first.

Although physical exhaustion may be a real issue for three- and four-year-olds, an abbreviated school day is also usual for the entering students in Japanese elementary schools. Before beginning the first grade, virtually all Japanese children have spent one, if not two, years attending preschool five hours a day or attending a day-care center eight hours a day. Nevertheless, during the first month of first grade the school day is reduced to two and a half hours because the boisterous, energetic six-year-olds are said to become too tired if they attend for a full day.

The exhaustion teachers are concerned about is more psychological than physical. Students are subject to considerable stress in trying to understand and adjust to the demands of the new surroundings. Yet for short periods they remain excited and interested in striving to adopt the more mature identity demanded in the classroom. By keeping the length of the school day within the children's ability to cope psychologically with the new expectations, their desire to perform well in the new situation is maintained. This calculated shortening of the period of participation so that children remain enthusiastic is characteristic of entrance to other Japanese early learning situations as well (Peak 1986).

During the first month of preschool the daily schedule is simple and predictable. All of the major routines of the preschool day are included from the very first day. On arrival in the morning, children individually greet the teacher and change into play clothes. They then play outdoors until about 10:00 A.M. After picking up their toys, they assemble in the classroom for morning greetings. Then they eat a snack together and change clothes in preparation for going home. After hearing a picture-card story or singing a few songs, they receive a sticker to put in their attendance books. The goodbye song ends the two-and-a-half-hour day, and the children leave to join their waiting mothers. This unvarying schedule and the teachers' attempts to follow the same routine each day undoubtedly provide a feeling of predictability and safety for the new students.

Meticulous observation of an unchanging daily routine is characteristic of other Japanese educational settings as well. The Japanese believe that rather than creating boredom or an overly rigid attitude, proper observance of routine is fundamental to moral and ethical behavior. Although there is plenty of variety in Japanese preschools once children have adjusted to the new environment, this variety takes place within the bounds of the carefully observed daily routine. Establishing and maintaining a routine is a means of training basic habits of daily life.

During the first few days of school most preschools have another teacher assisting in the new classes until the children become sufficiently accustomed to the routine that they begin to function as a group. Because most schools do not have teaching assistants or extra staff, this assistant is usually the director. She takes charge of children who have tantrums or lengthy crying jags, and she assists children who need help with the toilet if the teacher is otherwise occupied.

Although as director, the assistant may outrank the teacher by having as much as twenty years more teaching experience, she remains as unobtrusive as possible, never addressing the class as a whole and always focusing the children's attention on the regular teacher. Rather than patrolling the classroom and serving as an extra disciplinarian to correct inappropriate behavior, she stands with the children, acting as a model student. Only after the teacher has repeatedly cautioned a given child for inappropriate behavior will the assistant quietly reinforce the teacher's directions.

During the first month of school, as much time as possible is devoted to outdoor play, and very few organized games or content-oriented activities are presented. In all preschools studied, this practice was specifically mentioned as an important means of helping children negotiate the transition. Being outdoors was said to make the children feel cheerful and openhearted and to facilitate their adaptation to preschool life. *Yōji to hoiku* (Children and Child Care), a professional magazine for Japanese preschool teachers, gives the following advice in its April 1983 special issue on entering preschool:

The Outdoors Is a Place of Unexpected Discoveries

Some teachers, in an attempt to help their students become acclimated as soon as possible, have the children remain in the classroom and give them one toy or activity after another. But if you watch the children's faces when they are taken outside, there is an expression of relief and they become more openhearted. They react unexpectedly, watching older children's games or drying their tears when they discover a tricycle like they have at home.

Familiar equipment like the sandbox, swings, and slide, the rabbit cages, flower beds, and newly discovered insects provide a wonderful world of exciting things and show the teacher a side of the child's personality that is hidden in the classroom. During April [the first month of school] take your class outdoors as much as possible. (p. 50)

The shortened schedule and the emphasis on outdoor play are an attempt to lessen the psychological stress of the transition period. Children's attention is directed toward mastering the basic daily routine, the structure around which the other activities are arranged. Besides the predetermined routine and unvarying rituals, there are few dos and don'ts to be learned. These techniques give children experience in adapting to a structured life-style and help relieve the stress of the new surroundings and expectations through vigorous outdoor play.

TRAINING IN CLASSROOM ROUTINES

In both Tokyo Preschool and Mountain City Preschool, at the beginning of the year, a great deal of time and effort is focused on instructing children in classroom routines. From the first hour of the first day all of the primary routines of the preschool day are observed. Initially, accomplishing them is an arduous and time-consuming task for both the children and the teachers. The amount of time and energy invested in teaching these routines underlines their importance.

Classroom observations indicated that there are four primary techniques of training classroom routines: modeling correct behavior, reminding and instructing individual children, seconding student requests for appropriate behavior, and keeping the entire class waiting until the request is accomplished.

Different types of behavior modeling are used with different age groups of children. With older or more experienced children, modeling often involves a carefully staged demonstration and explanation of correct behavior. For example, on the fifth day of school at Tokyo Preschool the teacher of the four-year-olds demonstrated the proper method of washing hands. Observing that "from now on, we'll all want to wash our hands properly like this," she gave a demonstration at the classroom sink. Beginning by slowly and carefully pulling back the uniform sleeves to the middle of the forearm, and ending by shaking her dripping hands over the sink three times ("Count one, two, three") before turning them skyward as would a surgeon after scrubbing, she described and demonstrated each step in exaggerated detail. Children were then dismissed to go to the toilet, where the teacher stood near the sink, complimenting even partial attempts to imitate her demonstration.

During the first weeks of school, teachers generally consider three-year-olds too inexperienced in the classroom to profit much from this style of modeling. One teacher explained that initially most three-year-olds do not even realize that instructions addressed to "everyone" apply to "me." She believed that her students' behavior was more directly affected by their previously established habits and the example of other children seated next to them than by detailed explanations of rules and procedures. Therefore she attempted to set a proper and immediately visible example of the behavior desired of the students.

Modeling behavior is one of the functions of the assistant teacher during the first days of school. Listening carefully, standing at attention, or waiting with her hands on her knees, she is almost a caricature of the behavior expected of the children. The regular classroom teacher also demonstrates with her body the posture she wishes the children to adopt, whether by sitting down as she tells the children to take their seats or by standing at attention with her own hands folded as she instructs the class to prepare for morning greetings.

Another source of modeling is the behavior of other children. During the first days, the class shows a range of performance, from those who can barely approximate the routine to those who can follow it closely. The teacher encourages those who are less accomplished to approximate the behavior of the mean. For instance, to those who are not seated when they should be, she may note, "Everyone else is sitting down." Later in the year she will point out, "Everyone else is sitting with their backs straight," gradually moving the standard upward.

When modeling appropriate behavior, the teacher emphasizes that there is only one correct way to perform each of the daily routines. For example, proper sitting posture calls for a precise position of the head, back, feet, and hands. This posture is standard throughout the school. Children who can maintain proper posture are praised as "skillful" (*jōzu*) and "being able to do it" (*dekiru*).

This usage is not a conscious manipulation of language by the teachers but the standard means of praising another's activities, whatever the context, in Japanese. This cultural expression represents good behavior to the children as a moderately challenging skill they will be able to accomplish through effort and practice rather than as an indication of obedience or tractability. This approach removes the connotation of "bad child" from inappropriate behavior.

In fact, the injunction to "be good" (*ii ko ni shinasai*), which implies that a child who is behaving inappropriately is "bad," is rarely used in classrooms. Instead, teachers praise good behavior as skillful, at worst implying that improper behavior is clumsy and requires further practice. Hence children try to conform so as not to appear less competent than their friends. An "unskillful" child can easily redeem himself through minor exertion of effort. This technique is particularly effective in dealing with children who are at an age when they dislike being considered less skillful than their peers. It also fosters pride in children who perform properly.

Another means of training classroom routines is reminding and instructing individual children. Because it is believed to be difficult for very young children to respond to instructions addressed to a group, the younger the children, the more commonly individual reminders are used. The standard of expectations varies considerably for each child. A child who normally leaves his things scattered about on the floor will be reminded to hang up his hat, whereas one who normally hangs up his hat will be reminded to hang it properly (by the string, not the brim, with the right side out).

Japanese preschools set a high standard of order and uniformity as proper behavior. Each child, however, approaches this standard gradually, mastering it at his own pace. As the teacher of Mountain City Preschool's class of three-year-olds observed on the day of the entrance ceremony, "The beginning will be a little difficult for everyone. . . . Without overdoing it, I'll try to ask this much today and a little bit more tomorrow, never rushing and never stopping." Patience and optimism are the key to this process.

Teachers remain almost unbelievably cheerful and friendly throughout the training process. Punishment or sidelining of inattentive or noncompliant children was never observed, and even an irritated or loud tone of voice was extremely rare. If children did not comply, the teacher would repeat the request, as many as five or six times, then sometimes drop it, or she would stop what she was going to give the child gentle assistance in complying. In the classes of three-year-olds the most common method of training daily routines was this cheerful but almost inhumanly persistent litany of requests and reminders. It is a more patient and professional version of the training approach used by Japanese mothers.

Another subtle but ultimately highly effective technique of training appropriate behavior is to second student requests for appropriate behavior. When spontaneous comments from the children contribute to the goals or activity the teacher is encouraging, she immediately supports them. This technique is used both when children comment to neighbors who are behaving inappropriately and when they comment to the class at large. Often the teacher rephrases the comment somewhat more courteously as she repeats it: if a student shouts "Shut up" when the class is too noisy, the teacher may reply, "Yes, let's all be quiet."

This technique reinforces children's sense that pressure for appropriate behavior comes primarily from their peers rather than from the teacher. In addition, it capitalizes on children's desire for recognition and reinforces students who publicly urge others to behave appropriately. Seconding to encourage students to take responsibility for their classmates' behavior was used consistently in almost all of the classrooms visited. In the long term it plays a vital role in shaping peer dynamics to promote the internalization of classroom values.

The fourth means of training in classroom routines is to keep the entire class waiting until the teacher's request is accomplished. The daily routine and particularly the key transitional rituals are punctuated by moments when the entire class must wait, standing or sitting quietly at attention, for the teacher's cue to recite in unison before proceeding to the next activity. The teacher, smiling patiently, focuses the pressure of the attention of the waiting class on unprepared individuals until each child is ready to her satisfaction. Sometimes this wait may last five or more minutes.

Although holding up the class is actually an exercise of the teacher's authority and discretion, it is not represented to the students as such. Teachers remain relaxed and unthreatened, repeating patiently, "We can't start until everyone is ready." The implication is that not being able to proceed is a perfectly natural consequence of the group's unpreparedness. As one eloquent first-grade teacher in Tokyo explained to his class while keeping it waiting, "Without getting four good tires together, a car can't proceed. Without getting everyone together, our class can't proceed either. We've still got some flat tires in here."

The combination of the techniques of seconding and of keeping the class waiting is particularly effective. The ground rules of classroom procedure are structured from the first day such that the entire group cannot go on to the next activity until each child is in compliance. By suggesting that this delay is a natural consequence of the class's behavior rather than her own arbitrary decision, the teacher encourages the class to discipline itself instead of resenting her control. Thus, without an overt display of authority the reward structure of the classroom is designed so that compliance and the assumption of group responsibility for individual behavior is practically ensured. Individual challenges to this hidden structure end up being counterproductive, as we shall see in chapter 12.

The following transcript of seven minutes of classroom activity, from the second day of school in the three-year-olds' class at Mountain City Preschool, illustrates how these various training techniques work in combination. The class is just finishing the morning snack, which the children eat seated in chairs at low tables. The teacher and the director, standing in as assistant for the day, are also seated. The routine introduced the previous day is for the entire class to end the snack by sitting straight with hands folded and recite a three-part *itadakimashita* sequence in unison: "Lord Buddha, *itadakimashita*, teacher, *itadakimashita*, everyone, *itadakimashita*." Itadakimashita is a regional variation of *gochisōsama deshita*, a polite formula used at the end of mealtimes. (See page 92 for a description of this routine.) Unless otherwise noted, all teacher's remarks are made in a cheerful, friendly tone, barely audible above the voices of the children.

1. [*Shin, a boy, still eating, leaves the table carrying crackers.*]

2. Teacher: Oops, let's stay sitting down, okay?   [*Reminding an individual.*]

3. Shin: No.

4. Teacher: *[Teasing.]* Oh-oh, shall teacher take your crackers away?

5. Shin: No way!

6. Teacher: Of course not, so then let's eat them here. *[Indicates a chair.]*

7. *[Shin continues to wander.]*

8. Yukari: *Itadakimashita.* *[Leaves the table.]*

9. Teacher: Yukari, let's stay sitting down, okay?   *[Reminding an individual.]*

10. *[Yukari returns to the table.]*

11. Assistant: *[Stands up, takes Shin's hand, and leads him back to the table.]* Let's sit down to eat, okay?

12. *[Children begin to leave the table, some calling out* itadakimashita.]

13. Teacher: But where is everybody going? Let's play after we finish our snacks, okay? After our snack. I wonder if we'll have time to play. Ask me after we finish our snack. Ask me then, "Can we play?"

14. *[Children call out, "Can we play? Can we play?" and continue to wander around.]*   *[A reminder to exhibit appropriate behavior coupled with ignoring inappropriate behavior until the teacher is ready to have the whole class begin the transition to the next activity.]*

15. Teacher: It's time to go home.

16. Child: Time to go home?

17. Teacher: Yes. It's time to go home. So let's eat our snacks quickly.

18. Child: I'm already done.

19. Child: I'm done.   *[Individual bids for the teacher's attention.]*

20. Teacher: You're already done? If you're done, let's wait for everybody else. Some of our friends are still eating.   *[To eat at the correct speed and wait for companions to finish is a focus of table etiquette in preschools and elementary schools.]*

21. Child: I'm done, too.

22. Child: I still have a little left.

23. Child: I'm done.

24. Toshi: I want some more.

25. Teacher: *[To Toshi.]* It's all gone. Please go home and eat a *big* lunch.

26. Toshi: Okay, I'll eat *this* much. *[Throws arms open.]*

27. Teacher: *[To Toshi.]* You can eat *a lot*, can't you?

28. Child: I can too.

29. Child: I can too.

[Individual bids for the teacher's attention.]

30. Teacher: Let's see a picture-card story later.

31. Child: *Itadakimashita.* *[Another child leaves the table.]*

32. Teacher: Hey, hey. The people who have finished don't say *itadakimashita* and leave first.

33. Child: *Itadakimashita.*

34. Child: Lord Buddha, *itadaki-mashita*, Teacher, *itadakimashita.*

35. Teacher: Hey, let's all wait a minute. We're all going to say *itadakimashita* together, sitting at the table. Alright?

[Teachers explained that the new students as yet fail to under-stand that individual performance of a rou-tine does not suffice for proper group per-formance of it.]

36. Child: Lord Buddha, *itadaki-mashita*, Teacher, *itadakimashita*, everyone, *itadakimashita.*

37. Child: Lord Buddha, *itadaki-mashita*. *[Children are calling out individually. All but Hiroki have returned to the table.]*

38. Teacher: Hiroki, we're all going to say it together.

39. Child: Lord Buddha, *itadakimashita.*

40. Child: Teacher, *itadakimashita.*

41. Teacher: Yes, let's all do it together. *[Puts a hand on Hiroki's shoulder and leads him back to the table.]*

42. Child: *Itadakimashita.*

43. Teacher: The *jōzu* way to do it is to do it all together. *[Stands up at attention and folds hands.]*

    [Correct behavior is labeled jōzu, "skillful," not "good." The teacher models the desired posture.]

44. Child: Lord Buddha, *itadakimashita.*

45. Teacher: We'll all say it together.

[Most children have sat up straight and folded their hands; some are not paying attention and have not properly positioned their bodies.]

46. Teacher: We'll all do it together, okay? Let's fold our hands.

47. Assistant: *[To a boy who is not paying attention.]* Can you do it skillfully?

    [Inappropriate behavior labeled as "unskillful."]

48. Teacher: Wow! Everyone can do it really skillfully.

49. Child: I can, too!

    [Individual bids for the teacher's attention.]

50. Child: Me, too!

51. Teacher: *[To a child who has not folded his hands.]* Katsuaki too. *[He folds his hands.]*

    [Encouraging children not to be seen as less skillful than classmates.]

[All but two children are seated at attention with hands folded.]

52. Teacher: You're doing it properly too!

[Silence for a few seconds. Satoshi has his head down on the table. All others are now ready.]

53. Teacher: Okay. Wait until Satoshi can do it too.

    [Instead of reprimanding, the teacher brings pressure from the waiting class onto Satoshi.]

54. A boy nearby: *[To Satoshi.]* What's the matter with you?

55. Teacher: Yes. Let's fold our hands.

    [Seconding a classmate's reprimand.]

[Silence; all are ready except Satoshi, who doesn't raise his head. The assistant comes up beside him and puts her hands on his shoulders. He rolls his head back and forth on the table.]

56. Another boy: *[To Satoshi.]* Hurry up and do it.

[Children begin to fidget and break position.]

57. Teacher: Oh-oh! And just a
    minute ago we were all doing it
    so skillfully! Yukari, Chiaki, and
    Osamu are all doing it really
    skillfully.

    *[Using children's de-
    sire to be individually
    recognized as a model.]*

58. Child: Look at me!

59. Child: Hurry up!

60. Teacher: I wish we could hurry
    up and get this over with too.

    *[Seconding a stu-
    dent's appropriate
    sentiment.]*

61. Child: *[Screams.]* Hurry up!

*[More screams, blending into a high-pitched "Eeee!" Most of the class joins
in a long, loud, scream lasting thirty seconds.]*

*[Teacher and assistant remain silent, in
position with hands folded.]*

*[Not reacting to inap-
propriate behavior and
sentiment.]*

62. Child: That was neat!

63. Child: Wow!

64. Teacher: *[Cheerfully, but without
    smiling.]* Did I tell you to say
    "Eeee!"?

    *[Avoiding reprimand
    and soliciting stu-
    dents' opinion of their
    own behavior.]*

65. Child: No, you didn't.

66. Teacher: You're right. You won't
    say it any more, will you?

    *[Seconding appropri-
    ate behavior.]*

*[More screams—primarily Satoshi, joined by Yukari—lasting several
seconds.]*

67. Teacher: Satoshi, you've been
    acting strange for a while now. Is
    now the time to say "Eeee!"?

    *[A mild reprimand
    only after extended,
    willful misbehavior.]*

68. Assistant: Yukari, do you
    understand?

69. Teacher: We don't say "Eeee!"
    do we?

70. Satoshi: *Iya da* [a childish word of
    angry protest meaning "Don't!"
    or "I don't like this!"].

71. Satoshi: Eeee! *[Satoshi alone
    screams for ten seconds.]*

72. Teacher: *[Mildly.]* Is "Eeee!" the
    only word Satoshi can say? Just

    *[The teacher avoids
    making screaming an*

"Eeee!"? We're all going to say
itadakimashita together skillfully.

73. Satoshi: [*For three seconds.*] Eeee!

*issue of authority and
suggests Satoshi is
less skillful than
others.]*

74. Teacher: [*Still mildly.*] Satoshi, are
you listening? We're all waiting
for you. If you don't do it nicely,
none of us can do it. We all have
to wait for you. Let's do it
properly, okay?

*[Bringing the pressure
of all others to bear on
Satoshi again, only
more directly.]*

[*Yukari starts to leave the table.*]

75. Teacher: Yukari, I wonder where
you're going? Let's sit down
properly.

76. Assistant: [*To Yukari.*] Can you do
it properly?

77. Yukari: Yes, I can.

[*The class begins to break position. Satoshi starts to leave the table.*]

78. Teacher: Oh-oh. Things are
getting strange [*okashii, na*].
Satoshi, that's it. If you act like
that, we won't ever be able to go
home. Alright? Is that alright
with you?

*[Still avoiding forcing
compliance by au-
thority, but increas-
ing pressure from
waiting classmates.]*

[*Others start to leave the table. Satoshi runs around the room. The assistant
moves toward Satoshi. He hunches his body, refusing to be guided back to
the table.*]

79. Teacher: We can all stay seated,
can't we? We can all do it.

[*Kiyo lies down on the table and rolls around.*]

80. Teacher: Kiyo is acting strange.

81. Assistant: Kiyo *is* acting strange.

*[A bid for individual
recognition by the
teacher and other
students.]*

82. Teacher: Kiyo, let's do it nicely.
Let's sit properly.

83. Kiyo: Okay. [*Sits up and folds
hands.*]

84. Teacher: Koichi, let's hurry up so
that we can say *itadakimashita*.

85. Koichi: *Itadakimashita.*

86. Satoshi: *[Still not in seat, referring to a truck he played with earlier.]* Where's my truck?

[Satoshi shows by his interest in the truck that he doesn't understand that his behavior is keeping everyone waiting, so the teacher resorts to a mild exercise of authority.]

87. Teacher: *[Breaks position, moving to Satoshi's side and kneeling down to his eye level. Puts hands on his shoulders and says loudly and forcefully.]* Satoshi, listen to me! Now sit down properly! The truck is over there. Sit down properly!

88. Satoshi: Where?

89. Teacher: *[Pointing.]* Right over there. Now sit down properly!

[The teacher does not deny Satoshi's interest in the truck but uses authority to get compliance.]

90. Satoshi: I can't see it. *[Sits down and folds hands properly.]*

91. Teacher: *[Moves back to stand in position at head of class, folds hands. Speaks mildly to two boys not in position.]* Susumu, Katsuaki. Susumu, Katsuaki, Koichi.

92. Child: You're supposed to sit like this.

[An individual bid for attention.]

93. Teacher: That's right. Now we can all do it nicely.

[Seconding of proper behavior.]

94. Child: This is how to sit.

[Silence; all are sitting properly.]

95. Teacher: *[Carefully surveys the tables. Calls names of some who are not watching her attentively.]* Rumi, Kiyo, Koichi. Now we are doing it skillfully.

[The teacher is unthreatened and emphasizes the need for the whole group to wait quietly for the cue.]

96. Koichi: *[Closes eyes.]* Look at me!

[An individual bid for attention.]

97. Teacher: *[Still mildly.]* Hey, you! You have to do it properly. You have to do it right or else. Koichi, do it right, Lord Buddha is watching.

98. Child: Don't take a nap now!

99. Child: He's taking a nap!

[Giggles from the class.]

100. Teacher: Well, then, Koichi is the only one who'll be left out. Let's all do it together. Ready, go!

101. All: [*In unison.*] Lord Buddha, *itadakimashita*, Teacher, *itadakimashita*, everyone, *itadakimashita*.

[Inappropriate behavior portrayed as naturally isolating a child from the group.]

After the children had left, the incident was reviewed with the director, who had been acting as assistant. She observed that the children were so new to group life that they still had no "awareness of each other." Therefore they couldn't wait until everyone else was ready to leave the table or to say *itadakimashita*. Each did it alone, not yet understanding that in a *shūdan* (group) situation they must do it all together. She noted that children have to learn the distinction (*kejime*) between what is to be done individually and what is to be done as a group. She explained that the best way to teach three-year-olds this distinction is not through discussions but through training in appropriate forms or rituals.

Concerning the outbreak of screaming, she commented that when children have to wait a long time, "it comes out." She felt that her timing would have been different than the teacher's but that the exact moment to cue the class was something each teacher has to gauge for herself. At first, she explained, the trick is to get the children ready, and when they fall expectantly silent for even an instant, cue them briskly without hesitation. As the class gradually becomes more accomplished at the routine, the teacher can spend more time getting the class properly in position.

Although the teacher did not suggest this explanation, it also seems likely that the screaming was in part a means of relieving stress. This was the third such coming to order and group recitation required of the children that day and the second within a half hour. Hence it demanded considerable patience and a long period of waiting for children who were not yet "aware of each other" and were new to a group situation. Particularly for children such as Satoshi, the new routine and expectations were undoubtedly frustrating and confusing.

Clearly, Japanese teachers' initial task of socializing children in appropriate classroom routines is not easy. Slowly and patiently, a collection of novices must be molded into a cohesive group that can perform the many rituals and routines that make up the class day.

The task is difficult for the children too, as they try to understand and comply with the expectations of the new and different classroom situation.

Even comparatively young and inexperienced teachers are remarkably sophisticated in their understanding of children and surprisingly patient and unthreatened by inappropriate behavior. Thirty seconds of mass screaming failed to either disturb the teacher's calm tone of voice or cause her to move from the body position appropriate to *itadakimashita*.

A similar incident of mass table pounding was observed in another preschool. Later, the teacher commented that although three-year-olds are not yet mature enough to react to each other in a sophisticated social manner, the incident demonstrated that they had progressed to the point of being able to catch ideas from each other and were beginning to experience spontaneously the joy of combining their energies in a large group. She explained that making a big noise all together is simple, "primitive" fun and gives three-year-olds a sense of excitement similar to that which adults experience when singing in a large chorus or cheering for sports teams. What had appeared to me to be incidents of incipient mutiny calling for immediate and decisive teacher action were revealed as harmless expressions of impatience at waiting too long or simple enjoyment of rudimentary group activity.

Although incidents of interstudent competition are rarely described in Western observers' accounts of Japanese classrooms, this transcript suggests that at least at this early age, Japanese children vie strongly for the teacher's attention. This rivalry is expressed in numerous remarks, such as "I can, too" and "I'm done, too." This behavior is to be expected from children who have previously been accustomed to the virtually undivided attention of their mothers.

Competition for the teacher's attention is also expressed in ostentatiously appropriate behavior ("You're supposed to sit like this" [92]) and in calculatedly inappropriate behavior (Koichi's closing his eyes and saying "Look at me!" [96]). Without choosing favorites, teachers subtly manipulate children's desire for recognition, praising appropriate behavior ("Yukari, Chiaki, and Osamu are all doing it really skillfully" [57]) and encouraging noncompliant children to stretch their abilities ("Can you do it properly?" [76]).

The exact techniques and strategies of behavior control by which classroom routines and rituals should be inculcated are not discussed in the professional literature for Japanese preschool teachers. Beyond vague and general advice, such as "Accustom children to the daily habits of preschool life" or "Help children to understand how enjoyable preschool is," *Yōji to hoiku* is silent on the subject. When questioned about where teachers learn such techniques, both veteran directors and classroom teachers seemed puzzled. "Techniques? There is nothing special that we do," was a typical reply. When asked specifically about the four main techniques— modeling proper behavior, reminding individual children what to do, seconding student requests for appropriate behavior, and focusing pressure on individuals by keeping the entire class waiting— the only technique that teachers appeared to be aware that they used was reminding individuals of the desired behavior. The other techniques seem to be unself-conscious products of the teachers' own cultural background and classroom experience.

The process of adjusting to the routines and rituals of preschool is not an easy one. For some children, the cheerful, polite, but inexorable expectations constitute a heavy psychological burden. Not surprisingly, many children have difficulty in adjusting to preschool life, as part 4 will describe.

PART 4

ADJUSTMENT PROBLEMS

ems at Home

between Japanese children's lives at
nd routines of preschool life, it is not
n have trouble adapting to the new
st month of preschool passive with-
ns, and refusal to attend school are
will consider adjustment problems
in children's unwillingness to go to
n dropped off at preschool in the
ter we will examine problems mani-
ntrums, noncompliance, or difficulty
routine.

UNWILLINGNESS TO ATTEND PRESCHOOL

How common were adjustment problems among the new three-
and four-year-old students at Mountain City Preschool? In interviews sixteen mothers were asked to describe their children's initial
feelings about entering preschool, any changes in those feelings
and reactions over the first six weeks of school, and any problems
or difficulties they had encountered. From the mother's description
each child's adjustment was categorized as having been easy, somewhat difficult, or difficult.

Adjustment to preschool was scored as easy if during the first
six weeks the child had never cried or refused to go to preschool.
Three of the ten three-year-olds and three of the six four-year-olds
were characterized as having made an easy adjustment. Three of
the three-year-olds and one of the four-year-olds were classified as
having had a somewhat difficult adjustment period because they
cried or refused to go to preschool for at least one but no more than
six days. Four three-year-olds and two four-year-olds were consid-

ered to have had a difficult time adjusting because they cried or refused to go to school for seven days or longer.

This evidence suggests that adjustment problems were fairly
common among children at Mountain City Preschool. Two-thirds
of the children had experienced at least some difficulty, and one-
third of the children cried or refused to go to school for a week or
longer. Although the sample is too small for reliable comparison,
there appeared to be a tendency for four-year-olds to have less
trouble adjusting than three-year-olds. This observation agrees
with the professional opinion of the preschool teachers, who said
that new classes of four-year-olds are usually easier to manage than
new classes of three-year-olds.

The mother of a boy 3.2 years old when he entered preschool
recounted her son's easy adjustment:

> Preschool was a completely unknown world to him. Even though I
> tried to explain things a little bit, it seemed like he didn't really
> understand anything about what it would be like. After the school
> visitation day he started looking forward to going. Before school ac-
> tually started, he wanted to go in a general sort of way, but wasn't
> *really* keen about it. He wasn't counting the days like some kids do.
> *(How was the adjustment once he entered?)* He seemed to adjust pretty
> simply, with no difficulties. *(Was there a period when he didn't feel like
> going?)* No. He's never complained even once. After the first couple
> of weeks he started really looking forward to it each day. Every
> morning he'd start early, saying, "Hurry up, Mama, let's go." Then
> in a minute or two he'd say, "Is it time to put our shoes on yet?" All
> morning like that. So finally I taught him to watch the clock, and
> when the long hand gets to a certain place, then it's time to go. Even
> now he watches the clock every morning and calls, "It's almost time
> Mama, let's go." I guess you could say he adjusted pretty easily.

Another mother of a 3.4-year-old boy who experienced some
difficulty on entering preschool discussed his adjustment problems:

> *(How did Kiyonobu-kun feel about entering preschool?)* "He was really ex-
> cited. I told him, "Soon you're going to go to preschool every day.
> There's lots of friends to play with, and a nice teacher, and you're
> going to have a nice lunchbox, and they've got swings and a slide."
> He was really happy, and he wasn't at all nervous or resistant. *(After
> that, did he adapt pretty easily?)* On the fourth and fifth days of school
> he didn't want to go to school. *(What seemed to be the problem?)* Well,
> actually it was my fault, my fault entirely. You see, I never made him
> put on his clothes and things for himself, although I'm sure he could
> have if I'd made him practice. But I always did it for him. At pre-

school the teachers are training the children to do things for them-selves and so say, "Do it yourself." Which is what they should do.

Well, on the third day of school it seems that Kiyonobu came out of the toilet and his uniform smock was unbuttoned, and the teacher told him to button it. Apparently he tried a little by himself but couldn't and asked the teacher to do it. The teacher said, "Try some more by yourself." But it seems like he has this attitude that at home his mother always does it for him. So he said, "Teacher, you do it," and the teacher said, "I won't do it," and then he said "You do it" again, and they went back and forth a little bit. Then he said, "All right, I'll just stay unbuttoned like this until I go home." But the uni-form looks sloppy and funny hanging open like that. So the teacher said, "If you do that, all your friends will laugh at you," and he said, "I don't care if they laugh. I'm going to go home and tell Mama that you're being mean to me!" Actually I didn't learn this part of the story until about a month later at a parent-teacher conference.

When he came home that day, he said, "Today the teacher got mad at me." So I said, "You must have done something naughty for the teacher to get mad at you," and I asked what happened, but he's still too young to explain properly, and he just said, "Teacher got mad at me. I'm not going to preschool anymore." Anyway, the next day he wasn't too happy about getting ready, and at the preschool gate he wouldn't let go of me, crying "Mama, Mama." The teacher hurried over and helped separate him from me and hoisted him cry-ing up on her shoulder and started to carry him across the play-ground. Then he cried really loudly and screamed, "Help, help, I'm being kidnapped!" *[Laughs.]* Now where would he pick up a word like that? *[Laughs again.]* We had another difficult day the next day, and then the problem disappeared. Otherwise, he's always enjoyed going to preschool.

(Did you ask the teacher about the incident during the individual confer-ence in May?) Yes. Then I found out the story. At the time it hap-pened, I thought that I might write to the teacher in the mother-teacher message book that he carries back and forth each day. But then I thought he must have done something bad or the teacher wouldn't have gotten mad at him. And just because he did some-thing that needed a scolding, then if I write saying, "And then he came home saying this and that," it's really too persistent—the teachers are busy and have a lot of kids to deal with. So I thought I'd wait until the interview in May. They say that once or twice every child has something happen that makes him not want to go to pre-school. So I didn't think about it too much.

(What did you think when the teacher carried him away crying and he screamed "Help, help, I'm being kidnapped"?) I thought, well, he got scolded, so now he doesn't feel like going to preschool. As a parent, I felt a little sorry for him. That's because I think like a mother. I don't know if that's good or not. But after all, when it's your own child that's been born from your belly and you see him crying and calling

for help, you can't help but feel sorry. In other words, I'm not properly weaned from him yet. [*Laughs.*] I know what happened was the best for him, but still I felt sorry at the same time. I thought that maybe it was because I'd enrolled him at age three instead of waiting a little longer, and I regretted my decision. But that was only for about ten or twenty minutes. But that's what went through my mind at the time. Then I thought, Well, he's crying over a little thing today, but as soon as he gets over it, he'll start going to preschool happily again. And he did.

Although there had obviously been an incident at preschool that was serious enough to upset the child badly, the mother waited almost a month to ask the teacher about it. This reticence was typical of other women. The following mother, whose son had had a difficult transition to preschool, also had not discussed her child's problems with the teacher.

(*How did Shingo-kun feel about entering preschool?*) At first he didn't know what kind of a place it was. He went thinking that it was simply a big place to play with a lot of friends. The first day he went happily. After that he cried really hard every morning for about two weeks. When I'd try to put his uniform on him, he'd scream and cry and throw himself around the house like he was crazy. He'd try to escape and run from room to room boohooing, and I'd have to run after him and catch him and hold him down while I put his clothes on him. Nothing I could say would settle him down. I'd have to tie him forcibly into the bike seat. Sometimes the only way I could get him into his uniform in the morning was to lie to him, saying we were going to the supermarket. When I'd drop him off at preschool, he'd be crying, but after I left, it seems he'd always give up and go along with it. When I'd come to pick him up, he'd be smiling.

(*Do you think he was primarily unhappy about parting from you, or did he dislike preschool?*) I think he didn't like preschool. (*What do you think he didn't like about it?*) I wonder what it was? I didn't think about it too much. Probably being at home was more relaxing. After he gets up in the morning, he always watches television and hangs around all day. He probably didn't like to have to go whether he wanted to or not. At preschool he has to follow rules, and being one among so many people is tiring. Probably it was that, because he was used to pretty much doing what he wanted at home.

Japanese mothers and teachers clearly feel considerable reticence about discussing difficulties or problems with each other. This reticence exists despite many institutionalized vehicles for easy communication—the parent-teacher message book, brief greetings when dropping children off and picking them up each day, and both individual and whole-class mother-teacher meetings.

A great deal of detailed information concerning the child is exchanged through these channels. For example, some day-care centers require the mother to take her child's temperature each morning and record it in the message book along with a description of the child's morning bowel movement. In turn, the teacher records the characteristics of any bowel movements occurring at school and describes how well the child eats his lunch.

Although mothers and teachers frequently assert that they desire close and open communication, in fact problems are rarely discussed. Even when children have daily difficulties and frequent tantrums in class over a certain issue, such as dressing themselves, teachers rarely mention the problem to the mothers. Similarly, when children have obvious trouble adjusting to preschool, crying and refusing to attend, parents rarely discuss what happens at home frankly with the teacher. Both parties' preferred method of handling the situation is to hope that each will somehow notice the other's difficulty, either on parent observation day or when the mother drops the child off at school in the morning. Most wait for the problems to disappear of their own accord or raise the issue only obliquely in the parent-teacher conference after some weeks have passed.

During the first weeks of school the apparent purpose of the mother-teacher conference is to smooth the child's adjustment to the new setting. In fact, however, the vast majority of adjustment problems are never discussed between mother and teacher. The main reason probably involves Japanese cultural norms of interpersonal communication. Although the espoused goal of mother-teacher communication is the exchange of relevant information for the immediate benefit and assistance of the child, a more fundamental goal is the establishment of a positive and harmonious relationship between mother and teacher. In Japan issues that can lead to potential conflict are assiduously avoided in polite social relations. Although contact is frequent and cooperation is prized, person-to-person conversation is largely limited to well-defined, safely innocuous topics, such as the child's physical health or body temperature. Direct discussion of problems or interpersonal con-

flict is embarrassing and potentially threatening to the maintenance of long-term social harmony. Thus the espoused goal of
communicating frankly in order to assist the child's transition to
preschool is sacrificed to the more important goal of preserving social harmony between mother and teacher.

A handbook for teachers on dealing with "problem children" reflects the teacher's responsibility for maintaining a good mother-
teacher relationship (abridged slightly in translation):

> To maintain a good cooperative relationship between mothers and
> yourself, remember the following things:
>
> 1. The teacher's position is that of instructor to the child, but it is *not*
>   that of instructor to the parent. In particular, parents know more
>   about childrearing than you do. They also have broader life expe-
>   rience. As a teacher, your proper role is to work with the parent,
>   hoping that the child's development might proceed desirably.
>
> 2. Do not communicate with the mother about the things that the
>   child lacks to bring him up to the level of other children his age.
>   This is because mothers are very nervous about how their child is
>   seen by the teacher. If you say bad things, her maternal protective
>   instinct will be aroused, and she will feel that she must defend
>   her child from attack. Then she will not be able to confidently put
>   her child in your care. It is very important not to make mothers
>   feel anxious and insecure.
>
> 3. Do not try to instruct the mother or push her into your own im-
>   age of the ideal mother. Remember that the task of actually rais-
>   ing children does not go according to theory. Mothers are sur-
>   rounded by various difficult circumstances and are usually doing
>   their best. As a teacher, put yourself in their position, sympathize
>   with them, and try to encourage them.
>
> 4. The most important thing to remember each day as you care for
>   children is that each is a mother's irreplaceably precious existence
>   which is under your care. From the child's daily description of
>   your everyday actions, the mother will come to develop confi-
>   dence in you. (Ozawa, Nishikubo, and Kusunoki 1977, 26–29)

Another reason that frank mother-teacher communication about
problems is relatively rare is that most mothers and teachers appear to take a long-term view of the child's behavior. This attitude
is epitomized by one mother's comment: "He's crying over a little
thing today, but as soon as he gets over it, he'll start going to
preschool happily again." The general expectation that problems
would arise and eventually be solved was expressed in many dif-

ferent forms during the opening ceremony (see chapter 9). As the teacher remarked, "The beginning will be a little difficult for every-one—for you mothers and especially for the children. . . . Gradu-ally they will become accustomed to it." The director also stated: "I understand that new mothers will have many worries. . . . Don't worry if your child sometimes cries a bit at preschool. Learning to overcome difficulties makes children's hearts strong."

It requires considerable patience, optimism, and detachment to apply this classic advice to one's own child as each morning he must be forced screaming into a bicycle seat. In time, however, the problems eventually do disappear. By the third month all new stu-dents at Mountain City Preschool had adjusted to the new environ-ment and looked forward to attending preschool each morning.

SEPARATION ANXIETY

Given the importance attached to the mother-child bond during the preschool years in Japan, it is interesting that children's transi-tion problems are almost always described by their mothers as an initial dislike of preschool rather than as unhappiness at being away from home. Japanese teachers and childrearing experts con-cur that the primary problem is adjustment to *shūdan seikatsu*, not separation from the mother. Of the ten mothers interviewed whose children had at least some difficulty adjusting during the transi-tion, only one mother characterized the problem as being related to separation anxiety. Her response is noteworthy because she even-tually describes the separation problem as her own rather than as the child's:

> (*How did Rumi-chan adapt to preschool?*) She was fine except that she cried three or four times during the first week. Each day she was fine until we got to the preschool gate. Then she'd realize that I was going home and start crying. I was really surprised because I hadn't expected that she'd cry. She was so sad, so sad to see me go. As soon as I'd gone, it seems she always stopped crying and was okay again, but the moment of parting was really sorrowful for her. (*How was she those mornings when getting ready at home? Was she excited, or did she drag her feet?*) She was fine until after breakfast, but when it was time to start getting ready, she'd complain about this and that and say "Mama, stay with me." She'd push herself until she got to the school gate, but when it actually came to the moment of parting, she'd cry and cling to me.

(What would you say to her then?) Various things. I'd fib a little. I'd tell her I'd wait there for her, or to run off and play with her friends, but no matter what I told her, it didn't work. Sometimes there was nothing to do but have the teacher forcibly pull her away and carry her to the classroom. Other times she'd finally accept it and say through her tears, "Mama, be *sure* to come back and get me." During those four or five days she always went into preschool with tears streaming down her face.

(How did she get over it?) Well, her older brother, who's two years ahead of her and in the blue class, offered to walk her to school. It's just two blocks—you can see the preschool from our gate. That helped a lot. If I say goodbye at our front gate and she walks off with him, somehow she thinks that she's going off with her big brother rather than that I'm leaving her. After big brother started taking her, she didn't cry anymore. But when she comes home, she still looks almost overjoyed to see me and runs up to me, saying "Mommy!" These days she's gradually beginning to understand how enjoyable preschool is, so it's happening somewhat less than before, though.

(Do you think she cried because she felt sad at leaving you or because she disliked preschool?) I think it was the parting that was sad for her. *(How did you feel when she cried and didn't want to leave you at the preschool gate?)* I felt sad too. You know, she's my youngest and last child, and I have a strong feeling that I don't want to let go of her yet. When she's gone, then there's nobody left at home with me. *(How was it when your two older children went off to preschool?)* It was much easier. They weren't quite so attached to me. They adapted to preschool without a minute's difficulty. I was frankly happy to get them into preschool because I had three small children on my hands then, and I was ready to let go. With Rumi, she's my last, and although of course I'm glad she's enrolled, and she still has a perfect attendance record, I still kind of wanted to keep her at home. I'm much closer to her. You know, they always say one's youngest child is the most adorable. So I'm sure that somehow she can sense my feelings, and she knows somehow "Mama needs me," so she wants to do what she can to stay by my side. I'm sure she has that feeling somewhere in her mind.

It has frequently been reported that Japanese children rarely experience a separation from their mothers until they enter preschool. Much has been made of the supposed psychological impact of the reported practices of virtually never leaving the mother's side during the early years of life and never having been left in another's care (see Taniuchi 1982, among others). Unquestionably, paid baby sitters are rare in Japan, and it is a cultural ideal that mothers remain at home with their children during the early years. However, interviews with Mountain City Preschool mothers suggest that we may lack important information about the normative, as opposed to the ideal, child-care practices of Japanese mothers during the preschool years.

Almost all of the Mountain City Preschool's three- and four-year-old children had experienced numerous brief separations from their mothers by the time they entered preschool. Most mothers were straightforward and unapologetic about the fact that they often left their children to play at a friend's house if they had errands to do or so that the children could enjoy each other's companionship. Furthermore, almost all were in the habit of leaving their preschool children at home unattended to "watch the house" (*rusuban suru*) while they went to the supermarket or ran various errands for thirty minutes or so. At the extreme end of the spectrum among fourteen mothers queried was one who had recently taken a part-time job and routinely left her two children, ages four and seven, at home alone for two to three hours or dropped them off to play in a nearby park unsupervised if her brother's wife, who lived in the neighborhood, was unable to look in on them.

Of the fourteen three- and four-year-olds whose mothers were interviewed, only three had never been apart from their mother or resident grandmother before they entered preschool. Eleven were regularly left alone to mind the house while the mother ran errands. Four of these mothers qualified this statement by saying that they had only begun to do so recently, because they had felt that the child was too young to be left alone before he entered preschool. Their worry was not that the child might do something dangerous or forbidden during their absence but rather that he might become frightened or lonely and they would be unavailable to comfort him.

Twelve of the fourteen children had been left to play at another friend's house while their mother either ran errands or returned home. Two had been left at a temporary nursery room while their mother participated in various club or civic activities. It is clear that most of the children at Mountain City Preschool were already used to being apart from their mothers in the company of friends for several hours at a time.

Mountain City Preschool mothers were not unduly concerned about separation anxiety. They explained that if a child receives sufficient *amae*, he will feel secure about his relationship with his mother, and so brief separations will not be too difficult. If the mother tells her child that she will come back to pick him up, the child will trust the mother to return.

The strong bond of indulgence and trust Japanese mothers share with their preschool children undoubtedly provides a strong feeling of psychological security. Moreover, children's frequent experience of being left alone or in the care of others gives them first-hand knowledge that their mother will return. Usually the only precaution mothers who were interviewed felt necessary to take before their children entered preschool was to explain clearly to them that they would come back soon to pick them up. Mothers believed that the hardest part of entering preschool was adjustment to group life.

12

Problems in Adjusting
to Classroom Life

Analyzing classroom adjustment problems is somewhat more difficult than identifying reluctance to attend preschool. Part of the difficulty arises from the need to determine the difference between isolated incidents of inappropriate behavior and actual adjustment problems. Clearly, not every incident of inappropriate behavior constitutes an adjustment problem. For the purpose of this analysis, adjustment problems have been defined as consistently inappropriate patterns of behavior that reveal a fundamental incongruence between the child's feelings and attitudes and the most important rules of classroom life.

Japanese teachers are hesitant to label individuals as "problem children" (*mondai ji*). Instead, they prefer the gentler and less permanent term "children who require more care" (*te no kakaru kodomo*). In discussing such children, they go to extraordinary lengths to avoid implying that such a child willfully or defiantly misbehaves. Instead, they focus on the psychological dynamics of the child's well-intentioned inner feelings in interaction with his relationships to his family and preschool friends. Difficulty at preschool is assumed to stem from thwarted or excessively complicated expression of the child's good intentions.

A good teacher should learn to communicate intuitively with the child's inner self and guide the expression of his feelings into a more appropriate form. As a party to the communication breakdown, she must also share responsibility for the child's misbehavior. At all times the teacher must avoid developing an adversarial relationship with the child. A popular handbook for preschool teachers had this advice on dealing with "problem children" (abridged slightly in translation):

What Is a Problem Child?

"Problem children" are determined by the teacher's way of thinking about a child and her caretaking approach rather than by the child's own characteristics of behavior. "Problem children" are born through the relationship and interaction between the teacher and the child.

So as not to produce problem children, before deciding that a child is hard to manage, think deeply about your own disposition and personal approach. Why do you have difficulty taking care of this particular child? What is it about the child that you don't like? What things about the child get on your nerves? Why do your feelings of irritation arise? When you reflect on these things, you can see the child in a different light.

Before stopping a child's behavior or saying "This is bad," "You mustn't do this," understand why the child is acting as he does. Even if the child's behavior appears meaningless or illogical, realize that he is really doing his best to adapt to the situation and is relying on you as the teacher for help. (Ozawa, Nishikubo, and Kusunoki 1977, 10–14)

Japanese teachers' approach to children experiencing adjustment problems usually focuses on trying to understand their confused and unhappy feelings and going to considerable lengths to communicate with them. They avoid isolating or chastising children as much as possible. Rather than using their authority to force or coerce a child to exhibit proper behavior in the absence of a genuine desire to behave, Japanese teachers repeatedly explain to the child the behavior expected of him and arrange the environment so that through other agents he experiences the negative consequences of his own behavior. When Japanese children cry after inappropriate behavior at preschool, it is rarely due to having been punished or scolded by the teacher. Instead, crying results from having been forced to experience the consequences of an incident that the child instigated himself.

Another difficulty in analyzing inappropriate behavior hinges on the definition of what types of behavior are problematic. The behavior Japanese teachers consider particularly troublesome is different from that considered problematic when viewed from a different cultural standpoint. For example, among the behavior problems most troubling to American teachers are excessive noise and motor activity and hitting or fighting with other children. Japanese teachers are more concerned about overreliance on the teacher and nonparticipation in group activities. These differences in determining what type of behavior is troubling stem from cultural differences in the assumptions regarding the fundamental principles of social interaction and classroom life.

In this chapter I shall describe how Japanese preschool teachers deal with behavior patterns considered problematic in Japan as well as how they handle those considered problematic in the United States. I shall examine two typical adjustment problems that especially bother American teachers—hyperactivity and hitting. Then I shall consider two problems considered troubling to the Japanese—excessive reliance on the teacher and nonparticipation in group activities. Following these examples of the way in which some typical adjustment problems are managed, I shall review the primary means by which Japanese teachers deal with children's transition problems in general.

HYPERACTIVITY

Extremely active and noisy children are common in Japanese preschools but are not usually considered to present behavior problems. Teachers regard even the most fidgety and hyperactive children with an affectionate amusement similar to what Americans feel for adventurous, gamboling puppies. When the occasionally outrageous exploits of such a child are recounted to the other teachers over tea in the late afternoon, the teacher's description and the listeners' amused reactions are invariably filled with warmth and humor rather than irritation and anger. Teachers term these children "restless" (*ochitsuki ga nai*). Although they fall within the category of "children who require more care," they are not among the students Japanese teachers consider "problem children."

"Restless" children experience less conflict with the expectations of Japanese preschool life than may be the case in American schools. Japanese preschoolers are not expected to control their voices and their behavior except during the few brief, carefully delineated rituals that punctuate the school day. During the long play periods extremely high levels of noise and motor activity are not only tolerated but also cheerfully encouraged. Children are not cautioned against running, shouting, or demonstrating uncontrolled exuberance in the classroom. Indeed, we have seen that childish boisterousness and enthusiasm are believed to be an important source of character strength.

During the first weeks of school, outside of the brief moments of formal silence that accompany the transition rituals, a high noise level is cheerfully tolerated. This is true even during the supposedly quieter periods of the day, such as picture-card story time, roll call, and desk-based activity periods. The following is an excerpt from field notes taken on the seventh day of school in the class of four-year-olds at Tokyo Preschool:

> The children are seated at individual desks, and the teacher is standing at the front of the room. The previous day's opening ritual and roll call had been uneventful. The teacher remarked to me before class that the children were beginning to get a little bit used to preschool by this time.
>
> Immediately following the morning hello song, the teacher announces to the children that today they will use their new crayons to draw pictures after she calls roll. She asks, "Can you say *hai* nicely, in a loud voice, when your name is called?" She begins to call roll in seating order up and down the rows. One particularly active boy, near the top of the list, screams *hai* very loudly when his name is called. Giggles from the class. No response from the teacher. Approximately one child in three begins to copy him, screaming *hai* as loudly as possible. No response from the teacher.
>
> After five or six more screams, one girl says, "That's too loud." Teacher replies to the girl, "It is a little too loud, isn't it?" Another scream. The teacher says, "How energetic you are." Then two more particularly piercing screams in succession. Teacher says, "It makes your ears feel weird, doesn't it?"
>
> One boy has gotten out of his seat and is writing on the chalkboard. Teacher says, "If you aren't in your seat, you won't be able to draw pictures." Child returns to seat. She continued to call roll. After several screams she makes a grunting sound. One boy near the beginning of the list pulls his uniform smock up over his head like a ghost and leans almost out of his chair into the faces of the girls around him. They largely ignore him,.but one shows some irritation. She leaves her seat to go up to the teacher and says something not audible, pointing at the "ghost." Teacher interrupts roll call to say, "You can't see his face, can you?" As the girl returns to her seat, two boys get up and begin to write on the chalkboard. The teacher ignores them until she finishes calling roll (still amid screams). After the last child's name is called, she says, "Let's see which of these two boys can get back to his seat the fastest." The boys race grinning back to their seats. After all are seated, she says, "You have to stay in your seats," then begins to introduce the drawing activity.

Screaming during roll continued for about a week, until the children apparently tired of it. Teachers maintained their relaxed and unthreatened attitude and never explicitly asked the children to stop. Instead, they used more subtle techniques, such as seconding, discussed in chapter 10, to encourage the children to adopt appropriate limits for their own behavior.

In Japanese preschools the minimum standard for appropriate behavior that the teacher herself enforces is comparatively low. In this example the teacher corrected children only for not remaining in their seats. She either ignored other inappropriate behavior or indirectly encouraged the class to set its own limits. In particular, Japanese teachers avoid direct use of their authority to chastise or coerce individual children. Teachers correct only the most basic types of inappropriate behavior, thus preventing the establishment of a cycle of chastisement and rebellion between the teacher and a child. Tobin, Wu, and Davidson (1989, 23) in their discussion of Japanese day-care teachers' management of a noisy, excessively active boy also noted these techniques of avoiding chastisement for provocative or attention-getting acts as well as encouraging classmates to take responsibility for correcting his behavior.

HITTING

Although American teachers generally consider fighting and hitting other children a very serious type of misbehavior, Japanese teachers are comparatively undisturbed by these incidents. The occasional incidents that arise in the course of the day are usually ignored. When teachers do intervene, they are more concerned about reestablishing harmony between the two children by getting them to apologize to and forgive each other than they are with chastising or punishing the "offender."

The consensus among Japanese child-care professionals on the subject of children's fights is excellently summarized in a booklet for parents of preschool children distributed free of charge by the Tokyo Board of Education (1982, 25):

> Fights between children are an important experience in acquiring proper social attitudes and behavior [*shakaisei*]. Through fighting, children communicate their own needs and desires to others, come

to accept others' needs and desires, and learn the rules of child society.

If from the time that children are small, parents involve themselves too much, saying "Don't fight," "Play together nicely," and "Take turns," children are deprived of natural opportunities to bump up against each other. In that case, children come running to tattle, "So and so is teasing me." Doesn't it too often happen that the parents then take the child under their wing and solve the dispute?

When children fight, watch the fight and allow it to happen. Through fighting, children come to understand others' viewpoints and learn tolerance, self-restraint [*gaman*], and self-assertiveness [*jiko shuchō*]. It is important to raise your child so that he has plenty of experience in the normal fights that occur in everyday life.

Although Japanese teachers generally follow this advice, they do sometimes intervene in fights or incidents of hitting, particularly if children cry loudly or for a long time. The following incident from field notes recorded on the second day of class at Mountain City Preschool is typical of how teachers deal with minor incidents when they choose to involve themselves:

> Most of the children have come in from morning play period and are washing their hands and removing their hats, in preparation for a snack. One boy, Hiroki, still excited from the play period, twirls in circles with his arm outstretched and then deliberately wallops a nearby boy, Shin-chan, near the base of the neck. Shin-chan immediately breaks into loud wails, and Hiroki runs outside. The teacher, who saw the incident, calls as Hiroki leaves, "Hey, hey, you shouldn't hit people like that."
>
> Then, kneeling down to Shin-chan, who is crying loudly, she asks, "Where does it hurt?" Shin-chan rubs his neck, boohooing loudly, and she rubs the place lightly but makes no other remark. She goes outside to find Hiroki, who is twirling around the bars at the far end of the playground. She goes up to him and takes his hand, saying, "Your friend is crying. Now we're going to say that we're sorry." She leads him back into the classroom, where Shin-chan has stopped crying and is preparing for snack time.
>
> As they enter the classroom, the teacher says, "You were ashamed, so you ran outside to hide, didn't you? Then she leads Hiroki to stand in front of Shin-chan, saying to Hiroki, "You have to say you're sorry. Say 'I'm sorry.'" Hiroki says readily, "I'm sorry." Then the teacher says to Shin-chan, "Alright? Then tell him 'That's okay.'" Shin-chan replies, "That's okay." She then stands up, saying to the pair, "Well, come, it's time for a snack."

When hitting occurs in the context of a protracted disagreement, teachers almost never simply chastise the child who "put his hand out" first (*te o dasu*). Instead, the teacher asks the children questions focused on determining how the argument arose, to help each child put the other's behavior in perspective. Both sides are considered to be to some degree at fault, and often a mutual apology is elicited. Sometimes teachers ask other children to help describe what happened and, more rarely, to help resolve the dispute. Lewis (1984) provides an excellent description of an incident of peer management of a school yard fight. Although a child who hits another may be told, "You shouldn't hit other people," or urged, "Say it with your mouth," the act of hitting itself does not result in severe sanctions. Japanese teachers do not consider hitting as a "crime" or a demonstration of antisocial tendencies. Rather, it indicates social immaturity and frustration at an inability to verbalize one's feelings. These beliefs are particularly evident in the treatment of children for whom hitting is a consistent behavior pattern.

This portion of an interview with the teacher of the class of three-year-olds at Tokyo Preschool is typical of how preschool teachers describe the best way to approach children who hit others frequently:

(*What do you do when you have children who hit others a lot?*) Of course one brings it to their attention, but it's important to think of why the children do it. For example, perhaps they play most of the time with older children and so are used to a rougher give and take. In that case you say to the child, "It's nice you want to play, but this isn't your big brother, so don't punch or wallop your friends." If the child does it because he wants his own way [*wagamama*], you say, "Your friends are going to dislike you." Sometimes there are children whose personalities clash. Then the answer is not simply to separate them. You have to keep an eye on them and sometimes warn them if you see a situation developing. The teacher has to be very careful to remain aware of each child's feelings and attitudes. Children change a lot too, so you have to be careful not to think that a child who hits others in the beginning of the year will always be like that.

(*After there is an incident of hitting, what do you do?*) Tell the child that he shouldn't hit his friends and have him apologize. (*What about the child who was hit?*) Sometimes you have to smooth his feelings. Once in awhile, you can use the incident as an educational discussion to teach the whole class. Ask children what happened, who did what, and why. This helps children understand what kind of thing becomes the seed of a fight and that you shouldn't hit your friends. This is best done with the whole class, after the children who had the fight have cooled off. If you have a class discussion, it's always best to get it to end with the conclusion either that neither child was wrong or that both children were wrong.

Although teachers generally recommend that fights be followed by apologies, most incidents of hitting either do not come to the teacher's attention or are ignored. There is not a strong feeling that "victims" have a "right" to be protected from "aggression." There is an unspoken assumption that learning to live in society involves learning to live with friends who express themselves by hitting as well as with words. This theme is reflected in the management of children who hit others frequently.

The class of four-year-olds at Tokyo Preschool included one boy, Satoru, who hit other children at least three or four times during a normal classroom hour, usually for no apparent reason. On some days he was more excitable than on others. An excerpt from the field notes gives a sample of his behavior during such a period:

> The teacher is reading a picture-card story to the class. Satoru repeatedly pushes and hits the two girls and one boy next to him. They largely ignore him, but one seems about to complain after the sixth punch in a row. Teachers ignore the situation. Satoru gets out of his seat and begins to push and hit the children at the next table. The assistant teacher comes up to him, smiling, and puts her hands on his shoulders and pummels him playfully, trapping him and lightly punching him as he pulls away, as one roughhouses with a dog. She talks to him quietly meanwhile. The story continues. Satoru pulls out of the assistant's arms and spins back to his seat, hitting a girl alongside the face, and she cries briefly. The regular teacher interrupts the story to say, "If you do things that your friends don't like, your friends will cry," and continues the story. Satoru abandons his impulse to sit down and returns to the assistant teacher, hitting, twisting, and pushing her. She responds playfully. He then runs out of the room. The class continues, apparently unnoticing. After several minutes the story finishes, and the assistant teacher leaves the room to see where Satoru went.

The regular teacher explained Satoru's behavior this way:

> Satoru hits other children an unusual amount. He was like that from the beginning of the year—from the opening ceremony, in fact. He's like that because of his family background. He was raised with a lot of adult attention, but now he has a two-year-old brother. He's very much a mama's boy, but now she's busy with the younger one, so he's showing *amae* a lot. He is probably unhappy about his younger brother, and this feeling is reflected on the smaller children at preschool too. He pushes and pummels his friends as a way to play with them, but if he does that, he won't have friends for very long. It's dangerous, because if he gets labeled a bully [*ijimekko*] by them, he won't be able to get them to play with him. So we tell him about

that, and when he hits children, we tell him right then that he shouldn't do it and make him say he's sorry.

In fact, the teacher made Satoru apologize rather infrequently; most of his acts of hitting were ignored. The interview continued:

(*Have you discussed the hitting problem with Satoru's mother or written her about it in the message book?*) No, not yet. (*Will you discuss it with her during the mother-teacher conference?*) We'll see how the situation develops. Children can change a lot. (*Do you ever separate Satoru from the others when he hits them?*) No. [*Laughs.*] Satoru's problem is that he doesn't know how to relate to others [*sesshikata ga wakaranai*]. If we separate him, how would he ever learn? He's not a bad child. He wants friends, but he doesn't know how to get them. He needs more social contact, not less. (*Do you ever move his seat around?*) We keep a close eye on the children next to him. Sometimes they get discouraged because they're always getting hit. At the beginning of the year there was a very shy girl next to him who cried a lot when he hit her. We changed the seating there, because we were afraid she might start to dislike coming to preschool.

This teacher's analysis shows remarkable psychological sophistication and tolerance for a young woman with only two years of teaching experience and no background in clinical psychology. In fact, I was frequently given fresh insights into children's behavior (as well as my own) by the remarkable psychological intuition of Japanese preschool teachers. One incident the next year at Mountain City Preschool is particularly noteworthy in this context:

After several weeks of observation at Mountain City Preschool, Hiroshi, a burly, extremely energetic boy in the four-year-olds' class began running up to hit me several times each day. Striking me soundly in the stomach or the small of my back, he would race away again while I stood smiling vaguely, holding my pen and notebook, wondering what to do. Finally I settled on a plan of ignoring him, leaving it to the teacher to deal with it as she saw fit. The teacher appeared not to notice Hiroshi's behavior.

After several days Hiroshi's approach changed from a sound wallop to a swift, strong kick in the shins before he raced away. As his kicks became stronger and more painful, I began to regard his approach with caution and considerable distaste. After several days of this treatment an examination of my shins in the bath revealed five large, tender, purplish welts, each about the size of an American quarter. I spent the evening considering ways of bringing Hiroshi's "behavior problems" to the teacher's attention.

The next day, as another welt was added to my collection during morning play period, I glanced in the teacher's direction, relieved to see that she had noticed the incident. That afternoon I met with her for our regular discussion of the day's events. Wondering exactly when to broach the subject, I asked a number of unrelated questions at the beginning of the interview. Although I imagined myself to have been a discreetly invisible martyr, the teacher must have been able to discern my feelings.

Suddenly, in the midst of answering a general question on children's friendships, she remarked, in a way that made it obvious that her polite and obliquely styled reference was intended to refer to a different subject, "You know, every child is different in how he goes about making friends. Some children, like Rie [a precocious, sociable girl who often invited me to "eat" her mud pies at pretend tea parties], come up and smile and tug on one's hand and say 'Come to my house for tea.' [Rie in fact did this frequently, and I always found it irresistible.] Others, like Hiroshi, have just the same desire to make friends, but they aren't so sophisticated. Children like him want to play by playing chase. That's the simplest form of social interaction. Like little puppies, they come up and pounce and run away again and hope that you'll follow after. Later, they'll become able to say 'Let's play' with words."

I realized with a shock that to the teacher, the "behavior problem" was not Hiroshi but I myself, particularly my unfriendliness in rudely ignoring repeated direct invitations to play. Rueful and filled with admiration at the teacher's insight, I vowed to play chase at the next opportunity. The next day, before Hiroshi could follow through with his usual kick, I quickly put aside my notebook and pen and charged after him, making monster noises. His delighted squeals as we raced around the school yard made me realize that his "antisocial tendencies" had been a genuine invitation to play.

Thus we see that hitting is not considered a serious behavior problem in Japanese preschools. Normal fights afford a necessary experience in developing good social attitudes and mature interpersonal relations. Rather than being seen as evidence of violent or potentially antisocial tendencies, kicks and punches are believed to arise from immature but genuinely social impulses. The "cure" is not to isolate or punish children who hit but to strengthen their personal interconnectedness and foster their understanding of the social consequences of their action. Friends are also expected to develop a reasonable level of tolerance and understanding of these children's behavior. As Lewis (1984) has suggested, it is perhaps ultimately more effective to develop self-control through helping children realize that their inappropriate behavior has a negative impact on peer relationships than to make them fear incurring punishment from an adult authority.

Japanese ethnopsychology has a radically different conception of the origin and cure of violent behavior than does American folk psychology. The Japanese impute to hitting not an intent to harm but only a lack of maturity of expression. For this reason, hitting others does not strike at the heart of what the Japanese hold to be the fundamental tenets of preschool life. Comparatively speaking, overreliance on the teacher and refusal to participate in group activities are much more serious behavioral problems.

OVERRELIANCE ON THE TEACHER

Considering Japanese children's heavy reliance on their mothers, it is not surprising that during the first weeks of preschool some children expect too much attention and assistance from the teacher. Generally speaking, teachers are remarkably patient and willing to provide practical assistance to children who have difficulty in dressing, toileting, and performing other activities on their own. Some children, however, go too far, refusing to make an effort to do these things for themselves and expecting the teacher to provide the same degree of indulgent assistance and companionship they have learned to expect from their mothers at home.

Teachers are at pains to establish in children an attitude of self-reliance and a desire to try to perform these tasks by themselves. They also endeavor to turn the focus of the child's desire for companionship away from the teacher toward the other children. Preschoolers who cannot do this are said to be expecting their own way [*wagamama*] and to be showing too much *amae* toward the teacher. These children have failed to understand the fundamental difference between *shūdan seikatsu* and family life.

Teachers deal with such inappropriate expectations in a patient, low-key, but highly consistent manner. Primarily, they either turn a deaf ear to the child's requests or agree to help but busy themselves elsewhere, without actually rendering assistance until the child gives up and tries to do it for himself. Repeated encouragement ("Go ahead on your own"; "Try it yourself"; "Hang in there, you can do it") accompanies the teacher's slowness to assist. Teachers usually provide active assistance only after the child has honestly attempted to perform the task for himself or has been made to wait a long time for the teacher's help. They also give explicit instructions and praise as children gradually become more self-reliant. Teachers try not to chastise a child or hurt his feelings in this process. They are careful to render only a minimum of assistance, gradually decreasing the child's reliance on the teacher until he achieves independence and self-reliance.

Although for some children this approach is successful, others have an unusually strong expectation that they will be able to rely on the teacher, as they do their own mother, to perform the various routines of daily life. From their home experiences such children have come to expect that when it comes to a battle of perseverance, they will usually win.

Japanese teachers describe these children not as lazy or rebellious but as temporarily lacking the understanding that in pre-school one must do things for oneself. A common technique in these cases is to wait for an opportunity early in the transition period to plant the seed of such an understanding. This action usually takes the form of a protracted battle of persistence that the teacher, with smiles and infinite patience, inexorably wins. In these confrontations the teacher speaks no harsh words and inflicts no physical punishment but rather employs psychological intimidation through sheer willpower. Cheerfully patient instruction in the face of a tantrum is her weapon in the battle of persistence. (The consequences of one of these incidents, after which a child at Mountain City Preschool refused to go to school for two days, were related on pages 146–48.)

Several such confrontations were observed in classrooms. One, in which a child who consistently refused to do things for himself was made to try to put on his clothes alone, is reproduced here from the transcript of classroom activity on the fifth day of school in the three-year-olds' class at Mountain City Preschool. The children are supposed to be changing clothes in preparation to go home. Several who have difficulty doing this alone are playing here and there, making no move to put on their traveling smocks:

1. Teacher: Hey, I told you to get ready to go home. Why are some people getting ready and some people still playing? Tat-chan has gotten ready skillfully. [*To Katsuaki.*] Bring your brown

   [*Choosing as models children who have done what the teacher desires.*]

uniform. Do the parts that you
can do by yourself. Hang in there
when you do it. If you can't do it,
ask me "Please do it for me."
Nobuo-kun has done it nicely.

2. Katsuaki: I can't.

[*Katsuaki stands holding his uniform,
making no move to put it on. The teacher
ignores him, busy with several other requests to button uniforms.*]

[*Calculated slowness
to render help.*]

3. Katsuaki: I can't.

4. Teacher: If you can't do it, ask me
to do it. Say "Please do it for me."

5. Katsuaki: I can't.

6. Teacher: It's not something you
can't do. You *can.*

[*By asking for a for-
mal request, the
teacher indicates it is
the child's responsibil-
ity to dress himself.*]

7. Katsuaki: I can't. [*Tries ineffectually
to thrust his arms into the mass of
cloth.*]

8. Teacher: Katt-chan, that's not the
place to put your arms in. There's
somewhere proper to put your
arms in. Can you do it? Can you?

9. Katsuaki: Um.

10. Teacher: Um. Sure you can. Your
shoulder bag looks like it's in the
way.

[*A combination of en-
couragement and prac-
tical instruction.*]

11. Katsuaki: I'll put my shoulder bag
down and do it.

12. Teacher: Katt-chan, you can do it
yourself. You can.

[*The teacher busies herself with other children. Katsuaki pushes his arms ineffectually at the uniform several times, then it falls on the floor, where it lies
inside out. Katsuaki leaves and begins to play. After a minute or two the
teacher turns her attention again to Katsuaki, picks up his uniform—as it is,
inside out—and carries it to him.*]

13. Teacher: Can you put it on like
this?

[*Beginning of individ-
ual instruction.*]

14. Katsuaki: Yes.

15. Teacher: Is it ready to wear like
this?

16. Katsuaki: Yes. *[Holds out an arm for the teacher to put the smock on him.]*

17. Teacher: Katsuaki-kun, look. It's not ready to wear. Katsuaki. This is the inside. When it's like this. You can't put it on when it's inside out. Turn it right side out. To do that, you put your hand in here *[Puts her arm in sleeve.]* and grab right here. Now look closely. You're going to do it by yourself in a minute. Then pull it through like this. Now it's right side out. Katsuaki-kun, this is something you must do. This is not the job of your mother or people like that. This is your job that you yourself must do.

[The teacher takes the opportunity for extended teaching rather than quickly getting on with preparations for leaving.]

[She clearly explains that doing for himself is the main goal of the lesson.]

18. Katsuaki: Um.

19. Teacher: *[Turns uniform wrong side out again.]* Now you take your uniform. See how it's wrong side out? Put your hand here. *[Threads his arm in sleeve.]* Now who's going to do this next time? Katsuaki-kun. Right? Then turn it right side out. *[Assists him in turning one sleeve inside out.]* See, you can do it. Now you do this sleeve.

[Reiterates that the child must take responsibility and encourages him by helping him the first time.]

[Katsuaki looks elsewhere and makes no move to turn the sleeve right side out.]

20. Teacher: See, it's inside out. It won't work if it's inside out. Look, Katsuaki-kun. Look here. If you don't look, you can't do it.

[Katsuaki looks at the teacher's face instead of watching her demonstration.]

21. Teacher: Look here. *[Indicates sleeve.]* Right here. You can't do it because you weren't looking in the right place. Are you looking? Watch carefully. I'm going to turn it one more time, then you have

[Beginning of the "battle of perseverance." The teacher will not give in.]

to do it. Watch. You do it like
this. Okay?

*[The teacher slowly turns the sleeve right side out, but Katsuaki is watching
children playing nearby.]*

22. Teacher: You weren't watching,
    were you? Katsuaki-kun, that's it.
    It's your turn. Now you do it.
    What did I do? Show me. You
    do it.

23. Katsuaki: You did like this.
    [Threads hand inside sleeve.]

24. Teacher: That's right. Do it.

*[Katsuaki does not pull the sleeve inside out but instead attempts to hook
the sleeve over his shoulder.]*

25. Teacher: You weren't looking. Pull
    it through. Hold it tightly and
    pull it through.

[Katsuaki looks at the teacher's face and tries to pull, bunching the sleeve.]

26. Teacher: Look here.

*[The teacher touches Katsuaki's face, then
the sleeve, trying to direct his gaze at the
garment. Katsuaki stalls and looks around
the classroom.]*

*[The teacher tries to
get Katsuaki to watch
and try, but he re-
fuses, waiting for the
teacher to give up and
dress him.]*

27. Teacher: Where are you looking?
    Look here.

*[The teacher again touches his face, then
the sleeve. Still looking here and there,
Katsuaki pulls in irritation at the sleeve.]*

28. Teacher: It won't work if you do it
    like that. Watch me one more
    time. *[Turns sleeve of uniform.]*
    Now you do it.

*[Katsuaki stands before the teacher, who is
kneeling, holding the uniform. He makes
no move to touch the garment or turn
the sleeve and begins to look around the
classroom.]*

*[The teacher remains
patient and cheerful
despite Katsuaki's
now-total lack of
participation.]*

29. Teacher: Here, do it yourself.
    Take a hold here. Turn it inside
    out by pulling it all the way out.
    Use your hand.

[Katsuaki looks at the teacher's face and makes no move to touch the garment.]

30. Teacher: Take a hold here.

[The teacher shakes the garment slightly to indicate that Katsuaki should reach for it. Katsuaki tries to stand up to leave. The teacher pulls him back down.]

31. Teacher: Hey, hey, hey. You're going to have to do it yourself.

[Katsuaki tries ineffectually to hook the inside-out garment over his shoulder.]

32. Teacher: You're supposed to turn the sleeve right side out, not put it on. Weren't you watching?

33. Katsuaki: Don't look at me.　　　*[Meaning "Don't pressure me."]*

34. Teacher: I will look at you. How did I do it? Hold right here *[Puts his hand inside sleeve.]* Hold tightly. Now what did I do? Do it.

[Katsuaki goes limp and starts to cry.]　　*[A further attempt to escape the pressure.]*

35. Teacher: Okay. Cry if you like. You have to do it yourself. Or if you can't, say "Please do it for me."

36. Katsuaki: *[Boohooing.]* Mama, mama . . .

37. Teacher: You have to put it on by yourself. You've done it before. You can do it.

[Katsuaki gets up and runs to a corner of the classroom, where he stands with his eyes closed, crying. The teacher follows him, holding the smock. She kneels before him so that he's boxed into the corner.]　　*[Mothers report that if the child cries, they usually give in and help in dressing. The teacher, however, re-fuses to get irritated or to give in.]*

38. Try it again. One more time.

39. Katsuaki: *[Now wailing.]* Mama, mama . . .

40. Teacher: You have to do it. Turn the sleeve like you did before.

[Katsuaki makes no move to touch the garment.]

41. Teacher: Watch. *[Turns the sleeve for him.]*　　*[The teacher continues patient instruction al-*

42. Katsuaki: But that's inside out.

43. Teacher: No, it isn't. Now it's right side out.

44. Katsuaki: [*Wailing.*] Mama!

45. Teacher: See, on the inside are all of these things. [*Shows seam facings.*] Now put it on by yourself.

though Katsuaki is crying too hard to receive it.]

[*The teacher gives him the uniform and turns to the class, who have begun to wander in every direction.*]

46. It's not time to go out to your mothers yet. Everyone wait a little longer. [*To Katsuaki.*] You've still got a long way to go. Hang in there.

[*The teacher shows the child that she is friendly and supportive but will not give in.*]

47. Katsuaki: [*Crying.*] I can't.

48. Teacher: Yes, you can. Where do you put this arm through?

[*Katsuaki puts his arm out, waiting for the teacher to thread the uniform on it, still crying hard. The teacher holds the uniform open, and Katsuaki inserts one arm.*]

[*The teacher scales down her expectation at the first sign of cooperation but still demands a good-faith attempt at the task.*]

49. Teacher: Put it on.

[*The teacher drops the uniform so that it lays on his back, one arm in the sleeve. Katsuaki, still sobbing, holds his other arm out in front, waiting to be dressed.*]

50. Teacher: *Why* won't you do it for yourself? The other sleeve isn't out here. It's around in back.

51. Katsuaki: [*Tears running down his face.*] Where?

[*The teacher holds the back of the garment open for his searching hand.*]

52. Teacher: Here. Can you get it in? Hang in there. There it is.

53. Katsuaki: I did it!

54. Teacher: Now you've become able to do it!

55. Katsuaki: I did it all by myself! [*Smiles brightly through his tears.*]

[*Although the amount of self-assistance is small, it represents a breakthrough. The teacher's goal is accomplished.*]

56. Teacher: Yes, you did!

57. Katsuaki: I could do it!

58. Teacher: If you can do that so well, I wonder if you can handle buttons too?

59. Katsuaki: I can do buttons, too.

60. Teacher: Of course you can.

61. Katsuaki: Before I couldn't.

62. Teacher: You couldn't before, but because you tried hard, now you can. You did it all by yourself. That's because you tried to do it.

[The teacher encourages his new confidence, reiterating the main teaching goal.]

During her attempt to get Katsuaki to understand that dressing is a job that he must do for himself, the rest of the class had been abandoned. As there was no assistant teacher in the room, after the nine-minute incident many children had to be collected from the school yard and hallways where they had wandered.

Despite the intense pressure focused on Katsuaki, the teacher never once raised her voice or demonstrated any physical signs of impatience. She smilingly but unyieldingly demanded that Katsuaki make a good-faith attempt to put on his smock by himself. The degree of assistance she actually rendered was not the issue: the goal was to get Katsuaki to exert some effort himself. Katsuaki's feeling of joy at his new-found self-reliance demonstrated that a breakthrough had been made. As the teacher later described the incident:

> Because Katsuaki's mother always put on all of his clothes for him, Katsuaki didn't really understand that at preschool, this is something he has to do for himself. He also didn't have confidence that he could actually do it alone. I've been looking for a chance to help him understand these things. Today, although he cried, he finally actually tried to do things for himself, and he realized that if he tries, he can do things for himself. That's why he was happy. It's a big thing for him.

Thus overreliance on the teacher is one problem Japanese teachers consider important enough to bring children to the point of tears, if necessary, to overcome. Establishing in children a self-reliant (*jiritsu*) and independent (*jishu*) attitude is fundamental to creating a distinction between the *amae*-based world of the home and the group life of the preschool. Making a sincere effort to perform one's own tasks and master proper personal habits of daily life is a vital goal of *shūdan seikatsu.*

NONPARTICIPATION IN GROUP ACTIVITIES

Because of the strong emphasis on group activities in Japanese preschools, refusal to join in group activities is a comparatively serious form of inappropriate behavior. Nonparticipation can take two forms—passive withdrawal or refusal to stop playing to make a transition to the next activity. Nonparticipation is one of the most commonly discussed types of behavior problems in the professional literature for Japanese preschool teachers. Perhaps this attention is not only because group activities are a keystone of Japanese preschool life but also because unwillingness to participate is particularly threatening to preschool teachers, who are well-socialized members of Japanese group-oriented culture. In all preschools visited, it was a prominent reason for putting pressure on individual children.

The consensus among preschool teachers is that children who "don't yet understand the fun of being together with others" (*mina to issho ni iru tanoshisa ga wakaranai*) should not be forced to join in group activities. Rather, teachers should give these children a little time and wait for their natural interest in preschool activities and in being with other children to assert itself. This approach is clearly represented by the examples contained in a teacher's advice column in *Yōji to hoiku* (1983, 42):

Wait until He Becomes Acclimated

A-kun is a four-year-old boy who is not yet accustomed to the group.

Problem: A-kun comes to school in the morning and plays outdoors during morning play period. When it's time to come inside, he won't enter the classroom. Sometimes he will come if he is in the mood, but he usually complains and resists. . . .

Solution: It is best not to force this type of child to enter the classroom. Let him play outside as he likes. Sooner or later he will develop an interest in what is going on in the classroom. His interest will gradually draw him to join the other children. Be sure not to react to this child differently than you react to the others.

Stretch His Interest toward Something He Likes

H-kun is a four-year-old boy who will not participate in activities.

Problem: H-kun will come into the classroom, but then he sits down in a corner and will not move. He won't move from his sitting position when the group gets together for greetings or even for outdoor play. He won't sit in a chair, and because he won't go to the toilet, he usually wets his pants in the corner. At twenty-five kilos he is too heavy for me to lift. . . .

Solution: Give him crayons and drawing paper, and he will probably begin to draw. After he becomes comfortable with that, tell him, "It must be hard to draw like that," and bring him a chair. Gradually he will begin to participate in group activities and make friends.

In practice, the degree of pressure put on a reluctant child to get him to join in group activities largely depends on the activity the child is trying to avoid. Some activities, such as free play, story time, or desk-based activities, are not considered essential for the reluctant child to attend. Others, like the brief formal rituals surrounding morning greetings, daily goodbyes, and the beginning and end of meals, are virtually mandatory. If a child is unwilling to join the group for these activities, the teacher will exert considerable pressure on him to participate.

Following a number of direct requests, the teacher often tries to lead the child by the hand toward the activity. If this fails, she may warn the child that the group will proceed without him. Although to a properly socialized member of Japanese society such a warning is a serious sanction, this tactic frequently does not work with children who are new to preschool and have yet to "understand the fun of being together with others." Often during the first weeks of school the class ceremoniously proceeds without a reluctant member, who then happily returns to play.

If these tactics fail, the teacher may have to force the issue, provoking a tantrum, which she faces cheerfully, patiently, and sympathetically. Smiling, she psychologically outflanks the child, who ultimately finds himself the loser in this battle of perseverance. The following incident, which occurred on the second day of school at Mountain City Preschool, is typical of how preschool teachers dealt with repeated refusal to participate appropriately when they decided to make an issue of it. All are playing outdoors during morning play period. The teacher tells the children that it is time to go inside for morning greetings:

1. Teacher: Let's go into the
   classroom. Just for a few minutes.
   Let's go inside and say hello to
   Lord Buddha. Let's go into the
   classroom and all say good
   morning together.

[The teacher continues in this vein, approaching each child where he is play-ing. She comes to speak to Satoshi, who is still playing with trucks in the sand.]

2. Teacher: Let's go say good
   morning.

3. Satoshi: I don't want to [*iya da*].
   No [*iya*].

4. Teacher: Let's go.

[The teacher tries to guide him by her hand at the small of his back, but Sato-shi stiffens his body and breaks into tears.]

5. Satoshi: No! *Iya da, iya da, iya da!*

[The teacher tries to pick him up and carry him in, but Satoshi escapes and runs back to the toy trucks.]

6. Satoshi: I still want to play.

7. Teacher: You still want to play?   *[At the beginning of*
   Then play. Everyone's going   *the year, threatening*
   inside. You can play. All by   *to proceed without a*
   yourself. Okay? All by yourself.   *child usually does not*
   Goodbye.   *work because children*
                                         are not group-oriented
                                         enough to care.]

[The teacher turns and ostentatiously goes into the classroom with the last of the students. Satoshi plays alone for two or three minutes until the director, standing in as assistant teacher, comes out to the playground, where Satoshi is playing alone.]

8. Director: You're a good boy.   *[Flattery and coaxing*
   After we say good morning to   *used rather than a*
   everyone, we can play again.   *rule-based approach.*
   Okay? Everyone's waiting for   *The teacher does not*
   you.   *refer to principles such*
                                         as his refusal to come
                                         in.]

[Satoshi immediately starts to cry. He stiffens his body and resists the direc-tor's attempt to take him in her arms.]

9. Satoshi: No! *Iya da, iya da, iya da!*

10. Well, then, let's go and play
    inside for a minute and come

back. Come on, come on, just for
a minute. Let's say hello with all
our nice friends. Then we'll come
back outside and I'll play with
you.

11. Satoshi: No! *Iya da, iya da!*

[*Satoshi is now crying hard, his body
rigid. The director picks up Satoshi, who
begins to hit and pummel her. She carries
him gently but firmly to the shoe shelf,
where she sits on the stoop with him in
her lap. He continues to kick and hit her,
crying loudly.*]

[*The director treats
Satoshi's anger as in-
visible and makes no
move to defend herself
from his blows.*]

12. Director: Let's put our shoes on,
okay? Hey, hey. Put your shoes
on.

[*The director tries to put Satoshi's indoor
shoes on his feet, but he kicks at her. She
holds his ankles with her hands, and as he
kicks, she plays "push-me-pull-you" with
him.*]

[*Angry kicks and non-
cooperation are turned
into a harmless game.*]

13. Director: One, two. One, two.
You're really strong.

14. Satoshi: [*Still crying loudly.*] No!
Don't! *Iya da!*

15. Director: Look. Let's play together
as soon as we sing a nice song
with all our friends, okay? Don't
cry.

16. Satoshi: [*Boohooing.*] No!

17. Director: Why? Why? All your
nice friends are inside. It's lonely
out here.

[*Director's calm and
friendly but naive
questions make Sato-
shi's position appear
unreasonable.*]

[*Satoshi renews a frenzy of pummeling the director, crying "No! Iya da!"
again and again, hysterically. The director feigns sudden understanding.*]

18. Director: Okay, okay. Now I
understand. You want to play
some more? Okay. Let's play
together.

[*The director's sudden
capitulation leaves Sa-
toshi unable to enjoy
what he had wanted.
This tactic is called
"losing one to win
two."*]

[She carries the rigid, screaming child back to where he had been playing and sets him down. He lies stiffly against her, screaming iya da! *hysterically. She picks up a toy truck and rolls it back and forth.]*

19. Director: What shall we play? How shall we play? What shall I do?

[Satoshi continues to cry iya da! *and hits her ineffectually.]*

20. Director: I thought you wanted to play. Don't you want to play? *Iya da?* Then shall we go inside with our nice friends? That's *iya da* too? What shall we do? Huh? Are you okay? What's *iya da?* Aren't you feeling well?

[Satoshi's position is now made to seem ridiculous.]

[The director remains squatting, her arm around Satoshi, while he continues to cry hard for two or three minutes. She pats him and dries his face, saying "There, there" [yoshi, yoshi] and "Are you okay?" as he gradually calms down to hic-cupping sobs. He relaxes against her and she takes him in her arms. Still patting him and saying "There, there," she carries him to the door, where he can see the class. She stands in the doorway holding him while he continues to calm down. After the class has finished morning greet-ings and is starting to play, the teacher sets him on his feet.]

[The director con-tinues to be sympa-thetic and friendly, comforting Satoshi. Although Satoshi's anger is directed at her, she has neither said nor done any-thing that obviously thwarts him.]

21. Director: Let's say good morning to Lord Buddha.

22. Satoshi: No. *[Limp and unresisting.]*

23. Director: Let's say good morning, okay?

[Molding her body over Satoshi's, the director recites the routine greetings for him, bowing herself and thus forcing him to bow.]

[The child's refusal to cooperate is ignored, and he is made to ap-pear to comply.]

24. Director: Good morning, Lord Buddha. Good morning, teacher. Good morning, everyone.

25. Satoshi: *Iya. Iya da.*

[Satoshi seems about to cry again, but his resistance is weak. The director looks at him and laughs.]

[Laughter is directed at Satoshi because he is being ridiculous.]

26. Director: *Iya?* You still think it's *iya da?*

[The director laughs again as she picks Satoshi up and carries him to the shoe shelf and selects his shoes for him.]

27. Director: Here are your shoes.

28. Satoshi: *Iya da.*

[Satoshi picks up the shoes and throws them. The director, smiling, retrieves them and puts them in front of him again.]

[Anger and defiance again smilingly ignored.]

29. Director: Here they are.

30. Satoshi: *Iya da.*

[Satoshi throws the shoes again, harder. His teacher comes over and scoops him into her arms.]

31. Teacher: Now we can play again. Let's go outside, okay? What shall we play? Shall we play together?

[Once the crisis is over, the teacher flatters and humors Satoshi to restore his friendliness.]

[The teacher puts Satoshi's outdoor shoes on him, sets him down outside, and follows him across the playground, where she engages him in sand play.]

This method of dealing with children's direct refusals is common in Japanese preschools. Teachers maneuver themselves so that they do not appear to oppose the child directly, and they speak in a sympathetically supportive manner. Indirectly, however, they thwart the child, so that he gains neither the satisfaction of victory nor a clear view of who is opposing him. At the climax, the child faces a no-win situation, which has been made to seem patently ridiculous even to himself. There is nothing to do but rely on the friendly hand of support extended by the teacher, who then guides the child through the activity against which he had rebelled.

This highly sophisticated psychological outmaneuvering is common in many other areas of Japanese society—in families, elementary schools, and occupational settings. Without meeting anger, physical force, or even clearly defined opposition, the child inexplicably finds himself having to concede defeat. But who has brought him to this position? Certainly not the smiling director who hugs and comforts him and offers to play with him, nor the "nice friends" who are waiting to sing a song with him. This technique leaves the child without an opponent and therefore effectively undermines his rebellion.

The director further attenuates the child's rebellion by completely ignoring or co-opting his angry and defiant actions. If the child hits and pummels her, she smiles but gives no sign that she has been hit. If he kicks her, she plays push-me-pull-you, flattering the child that he is strong. If the child wants to remain on the playground, she first pretends not to understand, then acquiesces once the child has lost interest, pleading "What shall we play?" By pretending to misunderstand the issue the child is trying to articulate, his anger and defiance are rendered apparently causeless. Children soon learn that it is useless to rebel directly against the system.

This technique of dealing with rebellious children recalls a well-known Japanese folktale of Chinese origin. A mischievous monkey goes to extraordinary lengths to break rules and cause trouble for his superiors; he then runs away to a far-off land to be free of their authority. One day he awakens as if from a dream to realize that no matter where he goes, all of his actions take place in the palm of the Buddha's supportive and compassionate hand. Recognizing the impossibility of escape from authority, he returns home and accepts the rules he once hated.

This approach to managing angry defiance is institutionalized in other areas of Japanese culture, such as *aikidō*, a nonviolent form of self-defense. Although the practitioner can draw out the enemy, he must wait for the other to make the first aggressive move (as does the director [8]). Then he sidesteps the blow rather than blocking it or responding in kind [10–19]. The force of the missed blow leaves the enemy briefly off balance [20]. At that moment the practitioner catches the enemy in a hold that maintains his lack of balance, in clear contrast to the practitioner's own stability [20–24]. The enemy is now in his physical control and can be disarmed without violence.

Japanese preschool teachers do not use this disciplinary approach either self-consciously or calculatedly. Indeed, when asked about the techniques they use, they are unable to describe them and seem unaware of them. Their approach is a product of cultural patterning rather than a deliberately learned technique.

In this approach the teacher must maintain a friendly and sympathetic posture both during and after the crisis, so that the child will not be able to direct his anger toward her legitimately. As the director later explained regarding the incident with Satoshi:

> Satoshi still doesn't realize that at preschool you need to do things together with the group. Maybe today he began to get some idea. At the beginning many children have this problem. *(What do you usually do when children don't want to do what the group is doing?)* Well, wait for them a little bit. But it's best to let them watch what the rest of the group does even if they won't participate. At that moment they feel *iya da*, but through watching they will gradually understand how things are and later want to join. Today Satoshi cried and got pretty angry. But he wasn't angry when he went home. Children don't maintain anger for very long. They cry, and then they forget. But it's important not just to drop it as soon as they stop crying. It's important to cheer them up again. *(How do you do that?)* You can play nicely with them, bring them toys or something like that. If you make them cry, you shouldn't just leave it at that. Children aren't good at changing their own mood, so you have to help them feel happy again. We'll watch carefully how Satoshi feels when he comes tomorrow. If there seems to be some hard lump inside him, we'll try to help him understand that preschool is an enjoyable place. It's important that he not dislike preschool.

Japanese teachers see making restitution to children after they have become angry as an important ingredient in securing the child's friendliness and psychological affiliation with the preschool. To the Japanese mind, the issue is not whether this approach implies a softening of the teacher's expectations or a weakening of authority. Rather, it is whether the child wants to come to school again the next day. Ensuring each child's enjoyment of preschool is the crux of the means by which children are assisted in negotiating the transition period.

LEARNING TO LIKE PRESCHOOL

Japanese preschool teachers feel it is vital that their students like coming to preschool. On the surface, this attitude merely reflects a benevolent wish that the children pass the school day happily. But a much more fundamental issue is at stake. Japanese teachers' nonauthoritarian approach to discipline and training in appropriate behavior is ultimately based on the child's willingness to internalize the preschool's standards and expectations. As Lewis (1984, 82) insightfully notes, "When questioned about misbehavior, teachers frequently volunteered that enjoyment of school was the key element to good behavior for children. An emotional attachment to the teacher and friendships with children were considered critical elements in the child's enjoyment of school."

Enjoying preschool and feeling an emotional attachment to the teacher provide the psychological foundation for internalizing the school's values. The child must feel a strong desire to please the teacher and want to do his best to fulfill the expectations embedded in the preschool day. If the child develops an attitude of defiance or rebellion toward the teacher and the expectations of preschool life, Japanese teachers' nonauthoritarian techniques are rendered ineffective. Teachers are correct in identifying learning to enjoy coming to preschool as the indispensable first step in the process of adapting to school life.

Helping children "come to understand the fun of preschool life" (*yōchien no tanoshisa o wakaraseru*) is almost universally cited as the primary goal of instruction during the first month of preschool. The Ministry of Education's official guidelines for preschool education reflect the psychological importance of this period, as do the instructional objectives of Mountain City Preschool. Individual teachers frequently cite coming to dislike preschool as the most serious possible impediment to the child's preschool experience.

As Lewis notes, learning to enjoy preschool comes from two primary sources—an emotional attachment to the teacher and friendships with other children. During the first few weeks of the transition to preschool the teacher's role is the more important. Later, as children become acquainted and adjust to group life, friendships with other children assume the dominant role.

Yōji to hoiku gives this advice to teachers about how to help children better enjoy the first weeks of preschool:

Things the Teacher Should Bear in Mind
about Newly Entered Students

1. Let the child think that the teacher is on his side.

2. Take special care of children who are anxious or insecure.

3. Take the trouble to look at things from the child's eyes. It's best to put your eyes level with theirs as much as possible.

4. Before the first day of school, test yourself many times to be sure that you properly associate the names and photographs of the children. Know what name the child is called at home.

5. Give children plenty of "skinship" by holding them, giving them piggyback rides, and shaking their hands. Use dolls for greetings and formal phrases.

6. Play one-on-one games in which you talk to them. Make them feel that preschool is an enjoyable place.

7. Don't forget to be cheerful and smile all the time. Be sure that you call each child's name at least once before the students go home each day.

In the folk psychology of Japanese teachers a firm bond of trust and affection must be established between the child and the teacher and preschool environment before attempts to control the child's behavior will be effective. Until this trust is established, the teacher must try to avoid disciplining the child and must treat him as a special friend. This approach is reflected in the advice of the authors of a popular book for preschool teachers on how to deal with "problem children" (Ozawa, Nishikubo, and Kusunoki 1977, 87–90, abridged slightly in translation):

Problem: M is a four-year-old boy, whose younger brother is in the same class. With M as the leader, he and his brother cause trouble together a lot. M obstructs other children's play, hits and is rough, has difficulty playing calmly, climbs up to high and dangerous places, and throws rocks. His mother has raised the younger child at her side and hired a baby-sitter to look after M. Because of this, he is allowed to do whatever he pleases. Because of his rough behavior and style of play, other children don't play much with him; he plays mostly with his younger brother, and they haven't really established separate identities. The teacher feels nervous and irritated about M and warns him about his behavior, but there seems to be little effect.

Comment: If when she is around M the teacher has in her mind thoughts such as "There he goes again" or "He is really a troublesome kid," his behavior will get worse. It is important to develop a trusting relationship between the teacher and the child. To do this, look for M's good qualities. When you play with him, work hard to see him in the light of these good qualities.

Instead of scolding him, play sincerely and wholeheartedly with M. Then M will feel that the teacher likes him and will develop trust in her. Building on this base of trust, teach him slowly and patiently, without hurrying, about his selfish [*wagamama*] and willful [*katte*] behavior. It is because he hasn't learned the rules of group life that he behaves selfishly.

Ask his mother about his relationships with others at home, then tell her about his relationships at school. Then she will realize that her way of raising him needs to change. When talking with his mother, however, keep in in mind that childrearing is not easy, and remember her position and difficult circumstances when you talk.

Although the child's initial focus in developing a feeling of trust and security is on the teacher, friendships with other children soon become more important. Learning to enjoy being with the group forms the psychological foundation of preschool life. Mothers unanimously described their children's enjoyment of other children as the main reason they like preschool. The mother of the three-year-old boy who reported that she had to strap him forcibly into the bicycle seat to take him to preschool each morning (page 148) also described her son's eventual adjustment to preschool:

> (*What finally caused Shingo-kun to stop crying and start to like preschool?*) It was the other children and understanding the fun of playing with them. Slowly he started to mention some children's names, like Hiroshi-kun or Tomomi-chan. I still don't really know who these kids are, but he has several he regularly mentions doing this or that with. That's what finally made him happy about going to preschool.

Japanese preschool teachers see learning to enjoy other children as an inevitable process. By definition, there are no children in the school who are not one's "friends" (*otomodachi*). As the veteran director of Tokyo Preschool remarked, there are no children who honestly prefer solitary pursuits, only "those who don't yet understand the fun of playing with others." Learning to live in and enjoy life in a group is a natural and highly satisfying step in Japanese children's development toward social maturity.

Conclusions

I began this inquiry by asking how the "indulged" Japanese child becomes a well-disciplined student—more precisely, how Japanese children accomplish the transition from dependent and demanding behavior at home to obedient and self-reliant behavior in preschool. We have learned that the classroom teacher, not the mother, is the primary agent in the transition process. Japanese children do not undergo a radical personality change on entering preschool. Instead, they master a new, situationally specific repertoire of behavior, which renders them more tractable and self-reliant while they are at preschool. In preschool, children develop habits appropriate to *shūdan seikatsu*, which include self-reliance, conformity, and control of egoistic tendencies. At home, however, they continue to display the *amae*-based dependency and *wagamama* appropriate to intimate mother-child interaction.

Training in the habits and attitudes appropriate to group life is the most important goal of the preschool experience in the minds of Japanese parents and educators. Such attitudes include enthusiasm, openheartedness, enjoyment of being with other children, and identification with classroom standards of behavior. Appropriate behavior includes self-reliance, proper fulfillment of one's tasks, and observance of appropriate distinctions between formal and informal behavior.

This training is gradual. Before Japanese children enter preschool, they receive a number of increasingly structured views of the nature of the preschool environment, thereby developing a strong feeling of anticipation and a desire to become a part of preschool life. For entering students, the opening ceremony marks the transition to a new, more mature stage of childhood. Once preschool has begun, many children have difficulty adjusting to the demands of the new environment. Tantrums and refusal to attend school are common. However, mothers and teachers remain patient and unconcerned, confident that the children will eventually learn to enjoy preschool life.

Classroom training in group attitudes and behavior occurs indirectly, through accustoming children to the routine and schedule of the school day and inculcating habits and rituals of group life. Teachers attempt to make the first school days relaxing and enjoyable while establishing the most important rituals of the daily routine. With remarkable patience and tolerance, they slowly shape children toward proper behavior. The primary techniques in this process are modeling of appropriate behavior, reminders to individual children, seconding of children's spontaneous requests for appropriate behavior, and keeping the entire class waiting until the teacher's request is accomplished. Teachers avoid overt assertion of authority as much as possible, and most inappropriate behavior is simply ignored.

Sometimes teachers employ extraordinary measures, particularly with children who persistently display excessive dependence on the teacher or refuse to participate in group activities. In these situations teachers avoid the use of chastisement or overt authority. Instead, they prefer to outmaneuver the child psychologically and force him to realize that his behavior is counterproductive. Calmly and patiently they render a refusal to cooperate ineffective by not recognizing the child's rebellion.

Japanese preschool teachers are unshakably optimistic that sooner or later every child will come to "understand the fun of preschool life." Ensuring that children enjoy preschool is the primary means by which the internalization of classroom values is accomplished. Thus children learn the rules of *shūdan seikatsu* through a combination of nonauthoritarian behavior-molding techniques and the fostering of the child's own desire to adopt standards of classroom behavior. In this way Japanese children negotiate the transition from home to preschool life.

These conclusions concerning Japanese children's adjustment to preschool are germane to many other aspects of Japanese society. They shed light on Japanese family life, childrearing techniques, the establishment of the individual's psychological relationship to the group, the exercise of authority, and conflict management. They also encourage us to reflect on the way in which we as Americans socialize our own children. In the field of education and human development, Japanese children's transition from home to preschool life is an important window on the acquisition of Japanese culture. Although Japanese society is invariably described as group oriented, the actual experiences by which individual Japanese acquire this cultural trait have not previously been described. It seems clear that learning to go to school is the main arena in which contemporary Japanese receive their first lessons in group life. Mastering the unwritten code of preschool *shūdan seikatsu* is the foundation on which individuals receive more elaborated training in group behavior and attitudes throughout their lives.

In Japan group behavior is learned at preschool. It is primarily the teacher and classmates, not the mother, who teach children what it means to be a member of Japanese society. Group-oriented behavior and attitudes are acquired gradually through the implicit structure and expectations of the preschool environment. As Rohlen (1989, 22) notes, "The keys [to this training method] are patience, not discipline, and persuasive illustration, not rules."

Where do Japanese teachers learn these techniques for training children in *shūdan seikatsu?* The teachers themselves tend to be puzzled by this question. Typical answers are "We have no special techniques" and "We just try to help children learn to understand the fun of preschool life." Most of the techniques discussed in this book are discernable or remarkable only to outsiders; to the Japanese they are a natural part of daily life.

Japanese teachers readily admit that they learn a great deal about how to handle children through their own experience of teaching and through advice from senior colleagues. Yet this on-the-job training is not sufficient to explain why so much of the daily routine and behavior management in Japanese preschools appears to be similar throughout the country (Lewis 1989; Tobin, Wu, and Davidson 1989; Hendry 1987; Peak 1987). Japanese preschools certainly do exhibit differences in philosophy, activities, and style. Yet to the outsider these appear to be comparatively minor variations on a theme. Where do Japanese teachers learn what to say and do during the opening ceremony on the first day of school, or what criteria to use in teaching children to hang their uniforms up properly, or how to deal with a child who refuses to come inside with the rest of the class?

There is little systematic research on the training that Japanese preschool teachers receive in junior colleges. Yet instructors there assert that the instruction is largely theoretical and does not focus on practical issues, such as scripting an opening ceremony, or give recommendations about what to say and do when a child misbehaves in a particular way. Experts in Japanese child development and preschool education (Azuma 1989; Nagano 1983) concur that Japanese preschool teachers' training of children in *shūdan seikatsu* and management of their behavior are largely a product of their cultural repertoire and memories of their own experiences as students and members of society.

The techniques of training children in *shūdan seikatsu* observed in preschools are remarkably similar to those used in other areas of Japanese society, particularly law, government, and business management (Rohlen 1989). For example, Japanese businesses establish and maintain order in the workplace without overt displays of managerial authority by training employees in formal routines. These routinized habits strengthen the shared experience of the members of the group and keep managers from having to exercise their authority in all but the most important situations. Concerning the Japanese cultural technique of ordering society through the institutionalization of routine Rohlen (1989, 28–29) observes:

> Compliance with these basic routines defines one as a social being and a member of a group. To become part of a group does not require affirmation of a faith or the acceptance of a set of rules, but only compliance with the routines and a willingness to acknowledge their inherent necessity as part of *shūdan seikatsu.* . . . Failure to follow directions, careless variance from group norms and standards in such matters as uniforms, etiquette, and practice, for example, create surprising levels of consternation centering on issues of the offending individual's connectedness to the group. The result of such pressure is very high levels of orderly conduct in the organized spheres of society that do not depend on authoritative action. Participation, thus, not only signifies attachment, but represents a form of discipline.

Another Japanese cultural technique manifested in preschools is that of managing conflict by avoiding direct exercise of authority, using patience, compromise, and co-optation as much as possible. Rohlen (1989, 32, 35) describes this technique as applied in law and government:

> The practice is generally not to publicly acknowledge a divisive problem or conflict and then remove it to an objective, formal environment, as would be typical of a legal resolution in the Anglo-

American scheme, but rather to sidestep publicity if possible, to avoid direct intervention, to patiently seek compromise, and to ultimately knit the social fabric back together. . . . Patience, an emphasis on inclusiveness, the use of intimate relations, peer pressure, a reluctance to use power, and so forth, are all aspects of both [Japanese society at large and teachers' disciplinary techniques in preschools]. . . . It is not that central authorities lack adequate legal authority or are short of coercive power; the issue is one of not wanting to exercise that power because, unless fully justified, coercive actions ultimately undermine the entire system of affiliation and compliance. . . . The extreme caution about the application of power stems from the fact that these actions generate alienation in a system that is sensitized to mutuality as a relational matter. Re-attachment must be at least somewhat a voluntary act.

Japanese preschool teachers' reluctance to manage children's behavior by setting and enforcing rules and their emphasis on developing within each child a genuine affection for and enjoyment of preschool life are thus part of a larger cultural pattern of controlling behavior through affiliation and voluntary internalization of rules rather than through authoritarian enforcement of compliance.

It has frequently been observed that there is a great discrepancy between Japanese public (*soto*) and private (*uchi*) behavior. Japanese children's training in public behavior as a situationally appropriate skill helps us understand why this is so. From the first exposure to the greater demands for self-sufficiency and self-control in group life, children are made to realize that home and school are different and that these more restrictive expectations are appropriate to public group life. At home, culturally appropriate expression of intimacy continues to encourage the *amae*-based behavior. In this way the assumption of a polite, restrained, and positive social mask becomes a habit for Japanese.

In this process of socialization children are told that because they are a member of a group they must learn to control their egoistic and regressive tendencies. It is not the teacher but "all of your friends," "everyone else," or "group life" that places limits on children's desire to indulge their *amae*-based tendencies. Yet these friends are the same ones with whom children are encouraged to develop a strong attachment. Indeed, the presence of all of these friends is the main pleasure of preschool life.

In Japan the group is both the unsympathetic force to which the child's ego must submit and the primary source of companionship and fulfillment. It represents a diffuse and nonpersonified yet unassailable authority. In a more authoritarian tradition, such as that of the United States, children must ultimately submit their egoistic desires to the will of an authority figure or comply out of fear of punishment for infraction of a rule. The anger and ambivalance this process arouses in the child's mind has a clear target, which in fantasy and occasionally in real life may be escaped, resisted, or changed.

Japanese children soon learn, however, that to resist the system is to battle an army of friendly shadows. Authority resides with no one, and to change the collective habits of the group requires an impossible effort. To escape or rebel is to sever social contact with those who provide daily companionship and the warmth of social life. Perhaps because this identification occurs early in the child's life, Japanese exhibit higher levels of social order and less ambivalence toward authority than do Americans.

Yet it may be that there remains a deep-rooted element of strain in the individual's psychological relationship to the group in Japanese culture. At the same time that Japanese adults are profoundly uncomfortable when isolated from the social groups to which they belong, they also experience psychological tension in the effort to "keep one's wings pulled in." In comparison to the *amae*-based intimacy and informality of the home, even familiar outside social relationships cause some amount of *kizukare*, or psychological fatigue. To the Japanese, the group both beckons and binds. This tendency gives rise to a subtle ambivalence and a longing to return to the warm *amae* one has known as a child, a longing that follows Japanese throughout their lives.

Through the words of Japanese mothers and teachers and glimpses of their behavior toward children in various situations we have seen that their understanding of children's motives and actions is often different from that of Americans. It arises from different beliefs about the nature of individuals and interpersonal relationships. These beliefs in turn give rise to different recommendations for molding children's behavior.

This Japanese folk psychology provides a fascinating contrast to Western theories of the individual, his relationship to others, and the mechanisms of social control. In many ways our Western scientific study of child development has grown out of our own folk theories of psychology. Our culture's definition of preschool as a "learning environment" has placed a stronger emphasis on cognitive and intellectual development than on social maturation during the preschool years. Our assumption that public social behavior is primarily learned in the home has encouraged a neglect of how the child comes to understand and internalize the new expectations of classroom life.

It is to be hoped that the rich and sophisticated cultural heritage present in the folk wisdom of Japanese mothers and teachers will be elaborated by researchers and ethnographers and made accessible to Western society. It may be both undesirable and futile to hope that Americans become more like the Japanese (or vice versa), yet there is much that we can learn from each other. At the very least, understanding another culture can encourage us to reexamine our own cultural approaches and assumptions.

For example, American educators find classroom discipline to be a perennial and intractable problem. Many teachers in the United States feel helpless to control children's behavior at school because of what they believe to be inadequate discipline at home. We have seen that even though Japanese mothers' expectations for discipline at home are much less strict than those of teachers at preschool, Japanese teachers are able to work with large groups of children to achieve a comparatively high level of order at key points in the day through careful and explicit training in classroom routines. By investing much time and patience during the beginning of the year in establishing good classroom habits, Japanese teachers ultimately accomplish a great savings in the time and energy required for classroom management. Although these techniques may not work with all American students, they are worthy of serious consideration.

It is clear that the preschool experience teaches Japanese children the basic principles of social interaction that govern classroom and later public life. In the process they internalize the standards of group attitudes and behavior that make them members of Japanese culture. In this way learning to go to school in Japan represents the first step in the larger process of learning to become a member of Japanese society.

Appendix: Background
on Preschools as Institutions

There are two types of pre-primary schools in Japan: *yōchien*, usually translated as preschools or kindergartens, and *hoikuen*, usually translated as day-care centers or nursery schools. *Yōchien* are under the supervision of the Ministry of Education, Science, and Culture, whereas *hoikuen* are administered by the Ministry of Health and Welfare. The traditional definition of the purposes of these two institutions stresses their differences:

> The purpose of kindergarten [preschool] education was [at the time of its inception] to offer around a four-hour education every day to preschool children, three years old and above, in fostering their all-round physical and mental development. This basic concept of preschool education has been inherited to date. . . .
>
> The nursery school [day-care center] is defined as an institution for nursing children between the ages of zero to eighteen [months] for eight hours a day in principle upon the request of the parent/guardians who are unable to do so because of their employment or illness. . . .
>
> Since kindergarten and nursery school accept the children of the same age groups, . . . the Ministry of Education, Science, and Culture and the Ministry of Health and Welfare had a consultation in 1963, and reached the following agreement:
>
> a. The two institutions have clear divisions of work. The kindergarten aims at providing school education to children while nursery school nurses children who cannot receive enough care at home due to some reasons. (Education of course is included as an indispensable part of nursing in nursery school.)
>
> b. Of the various activities organized by the nursery school, it is desirable for the nursery school to be based on the Curriculum Standards for Kindergarten when it undertakes educational activities. This applies only to children in the same age groups as those of kindergarten-going children. (Kodama 1983, 1, 3, 9)

As officially prescribed, the same basic curriculum is used in both institutions. In practice, except for the age groups served, the

194   *Appendix*

Table 2 Number of Public and Private Preschools
and Day-Care Centers in Japan (1988)

Institution	National Public	Local Public	Private	Total
Preschools	48	6,251	8,816	15,115
Day-care centers	0	13,463	9,318	22,781

Sources: For preschools, Monbushō 1988, 402–4. For day-care centers, Kōseishō 1990, 295 (1988 data).

duration of the school day, and the criterion regarding maternal employment, the two institutions are more similar than different. For example, the daily routines that comprise the school day, the types of common activities, and the teachers' style of managing children's behavior are similar. Furthermore, the competition to attract enrollment has encouraged many private preschools to adopt those characteristics of day-care centers that serve to increase the preschool's appeal to parents, and day-care centers have borrowed some aspects of preschools. For example, some preschools offer an optional after-school activities program designed to care for children until 5:00 P.M., and many day-care centers offer a curriculum that is educational rather than strictly custodial.

Both preschools and day-care centers in Japan may be either public or private. Most preschools are privately established, whereas most day-care centers are public (Table 2). Three quarters of private preschools are established by "school juridical persons," legal entities whose primary purpose is the establishment of a school; the remainder are founded by private individuals (13 percent) or religious organizations (11 percent) (Monbushō 1988, 404–5). Public preschools are of two types: a small number are national public institutions attached as laboratory schools to national universities; many more are local public institutions established by municipal and prefectural authorities.

Although day-care centers are more numerous than preschools, they enroll a smaller percentage of the pre-primary-school age group. While the ratio of preschools to day-care centers is approximately two to three, the ratio of three-, four-, and five-year-olds enrolled in preschools to those enrolled in day-care centers is the inverse, three to two (Table 3).

More than 90 percent of Japanese four- and five-year-olds are

Table 3   Enrollment in Preschools and Day-Care Centers as
a Percentage of the Population, Ages 0–5 (1988)

Age	Number of Children in Cohort	Preschool Enrollment	Percentage of Cohort in Preschool	Day-Care Enrollment	Percentage of Cohort in Day Care	Percentage of Cohort in Pre-Primary Schools
0	1,316,000	—	—	54,575	4.1	4.1
1	1,360,000	—	—	361,982[a]	13.2	13.2
2	1,383,000	—	—			
3	1,422,000	246,770	13.3	421,286	29.6	42.9
4	1,484,000	827,690	54.2	946,960[a]	31.7	91.8
5	1,501,000	967,360	65.8			

Sources: For preschools, Monbushō 1988, 412–14. For day-care centers, Kōseishō 1990, 295 (1988 data).
[a]The Ministry of Welfare supplies only aggregated statistics for these age groups.

enrolled in pre-primary schools. Unfortunately, because the Ministry of Welfare provides only aggregate statistics for these cohorts, it is difficult to ascertain the precise percentage of children who have one, two, or three years of pre-primary-school experience. However, first-grade teachers and principals report that there are virtually no children who have not had at least one year of preschool and that almost all children have had at least two years.

Boocock (1989) has noted that besides the licensed preschool and day-care centers reported by the Ministries of Education and Welfare there is an undetermined but substantial number of unlicensed institutions. If enrollments in these institutions could be added to those shown in Table 3, more than 91 percent of all four- and five-year-olds would be enrolled.

During the past fifteen years enrollment of three-year-olds has grown steadily. The percentage of Japanese three-year-olds enrolled in either preschool or day-care centers had risen from 25.7 percent in 1976 to 43 percent in 1988. This trend is expected to continue. The choice faced by Japanese mothers is not whether to enroll their child in a pre-primary school but whether to enroll him for two or for three years.

Table 3 also chronicles the declining number of children in the preschool age group. Each year since 1974 the annual census has reported a drop in the number of births (Statistics Bureau 1989, 25). This decline has created a worsening financial situation for many

Table 4   Number of Preschools Enrolling Children of Various Ages (1988)

	All Preschools	National Public	Local Public	Private
Total	14,906	48	6,182	8,676
3-, 4-, and 5-year-olds	8,497	44	258	8,195
4- and 5-year-olds	4,247	4	3,820	423
5-year-olds only	2,116	0	2,091	25
3- and 4-year-olds	24	0	1	23
3- and 5-year-olds	6	0	3	3
4-year-olds only	12	0	8	4
3-year-olds only	4	0	1	3

Source: Monbushō 1988, 407.

private preschools. Many have found it necessary to offer classes for younger age groups, increase the uniqueness of their program, or offer special benefits, such as after-school day care or bus transportation, to attract additional students.

Private preschools have been the leaders in facilitating the enrollment of three-year-olds. Comparatively few local public preschools offer classes for three-year-olds, and almost one-third offer classes for five-year-olds only (Table 4). The continued existence of a substantial number of local public preschools enrolling only five-year-olds is the main reason that 10 percent fewer four-year-olds than five-year-olds are enrolled in preschools (see Table 3). Except at these few public preschools, two or three years of pre-primary-school attendance is standard throughout Japan. This discrepancy between the age at which children usually enroll in local public preschools and the age at which they enroll in other preschool institutions is graphically demonstrated by Ministry of Education statistics on the enrollment history of the 1988 five-year-old cohort (Table 5).

According to the principal of a Tokyo-area public preschool for five-year-olds only, the reason that many public preschools enroll only five-year-olds is related to the decline in the population of pre-school-age children. The ever-shrinking pool of enrollees has created financial difficulties for many private preschools that cannot meet desired enrollment quotas. Public preschools are usually attractive to parents because they are less expensive. An informal policy for "peaceful coexistence" between the city's public and pri-

Table 5   Age at Which Five-Year-Olds First Enrolled in Preschool (1988)

| Type of Preschool | Age at First Enrollment | | | | | | Total Number of Five-Year-Olds Enrolled in Each Type of Institution |
| | Three Years Old | | Four Years Old | | Five Years Old | | |
	Number of Students	Percentage of Five-Year-Old Class	Number of Students	Percentage of Five-Year-Old Class	Number of Students	Percentage of Five-Year-Old Class	
National public	904	32.7	1,844	66.8	13	0.5	2,761
Local public	4,743	1.6	154,956	52.2	137,072	46.2	296,771
Private	195,672	29.3	434,437	65.0	37,719	5.7	667,828
All types combined	201,319	20.8	591,237	61.1	174,804	18.1	967,360

Source: Monbushō 1988, 412–23.

Table 6   Average Number of Classes and Students per Preschool (1988)

Type of Preschool	Number of Classes per Preschool		Number of Students per Preschool	
	Mean	Mode	Mean	Mode
National public	4.6	5	138	151–200
Local public	2.8	2	75	1–50
Private	6.2	3, 5[a]	178	101–150
All types	4.8	2	135	51–100

Source: Monbushō 1988, 406–07, 409–10.
  [a] Bimodal.

Table 7   Average Annual Household Preschool-Related Expenditures per Preschool Child (1987)

Preschool-Related Expenditures	Local Public Preschool	Private Preschool
Tuition	¥55,250	¥132,264
School meals	11,348	15,263
Transportation	10,015	20,609
Books and supplies	9,350	10,988
P.T.A. fees	4,229	4,583
Extracurricular activity fees	1,496	2,800
Contributions	279	687
Health	219	475
Other	13,823	43,681
Totals	¥106,009	¥231,350

Source: Statistics Bureau, Management and Coordination Agency, Japan 1989.

vate preschools included the understanding that public preschools would limit themselves to enrolling five-year-olds. This restriction benefited private preschools by encouraging parents who wished their children to have more than one year of preschool experience to choose a private preschool. It also benefited public institutions, which now did not have to hire and tenure public employees as teachers of three- and four-year-old students, who later might not be needed because of the expected continuing decline in the birthrate.

The number of classes and students in each school depends on the size of the facility and the number of children in a given neighborhood. Private preschools are usually at least twice as large as local public preschools. Because of the declining birthrate many preschools are not filled to capacity. The typical preschool has about 135 children, divided into four or five classes. The mode is somewhat smaller, owing to the large number of small local public preschools (Table 6).

Neither public nor private preschools are free of charge. Although both are subsidized by the national and prefectural governments (Kodama 1983, 3), parents must pay a substantial amount in tuition and fees. In 1987 the average annual cost of attending a local public preschool was ¥106,009, as opposed to ¥231,350 for a private preschool, or about $815 and $1780 at an exchange rate of 130 yen per US dollar, respectively (Table 7). The fact that despite the cost almost all Japanese parents send their children to two years of preschool attests to the high value placed on pre-primary-school education.

References

Azuma, Hiroshi. 1989. Personal communication, letter dated September 12.

Bedford, Leslie. 1979. Rakuto Kindergarten: Observations on Japanese Preschooling. *Harvard Graduate School of Education Association Bulletin* 23 (Spring): 18–20.

Benedict, R. 1946. *The Chrysanthemum and the Sword.* Boston: Houghton Mifflin.

Beardsley, R., J. Hall, and R. Ward. 1959. *Village Japan.* Chicago: University of Chicago Press.

Bingham, N. 1978–79. Infant Day Care in Japan: Possible Developmental Implications. *Annual Report of the Faculty of Education, Hokkaido University,* 55–73.

Boocock, Sarane. 1989. Controlled Diversity: An Overview of the Japanese Preschool System. *Journal of Japanese Studies* 15, no. 1 (Winter): 41–56.

Carmichael, L., and R. Carmichael. 1972. Observations of the Behavior of Japanese Kindergarten Children. *Psychologia* 15: 41–65.

Caudill, William. 1976. The Cultural and Interpersonal Context of Everyday Health and Illness in Japan and America. In *Asian Medical Systems,* ed. Charles Leslie. Berkeley and Los Angeles: University of California Press.

Conroy, M., R. Hess, H. Azuma, and K. Kashiwagi. 1980. Maternal Strategies for Regulating Children's Behavior: Japanese and American Families. *Journal of Cross-Cultural Psychology* 11, no. 2 (June): 153–72.

DeVos, G. 1963. Deviancy and Social Change: A Psychocultural Evaluation of Trends in Japanese Delinquency and Suicide. In *Japanese Culture: Its Development and Characteristics,* ed. R. Smith and R. Beardsley. Chicago: Aldine.

———. 1973. *Socialization for Achievement.* Berkeley and Los Angeles: University of California Press.

DeVos, G., and E. Murakami. 1974. Violence and Aggression in Fantasy: A Comparison of American and Japanese Lower-Class Youth. In *Mental Health Research in Asia and the Pacific,* vol. 3, *Youth, Socialization, and Mental Health,* ed. W. Lebra. Honolulu: University Press of Hawaii.

Doi, T. 1973. *The Anatomy of Dependence.* Tokyo: Kodansha.

Embree, J. 1939. *Suye Mura: A Japanese Village.* Chicago: University of Chicago Press.

Hendry, Joy. 1986a. *Becoming Japanese: The World of the Preschool Child.* Honolulu: University of Hawaii Press.

———. 1986b. Kindergartens and the Transition from Home to School Education. *Comparative Education* 22: 53–58.

Kodama, Taketoshi. 1983. *Preschool Education in Japan*. NIER Occasional Paper. Tokyo: National Institute for Educational Research, March.

Kōseishō (Japanese Ministry of Health and Welfare). 1990. *1989 Annual Report on Health and Welfare*. Tokyo: Kōseishō.

Kumagai, H. 1981. A Dissection of Intimacy: A Study of "Bipolar Posturing" in Japanese Social Interaction—*Amaeru* and *Amayakasu*, Indulgence, and Deference. *Culture, Medicine, and Psychiatry* 5: 249–72.

Lanham, B. 1956. Aspects of Child Care in Japan: Preliminary Report. In *Personal Character and Cultural Milieu*, ed. D. Haring. Syracuse, N.Y.: Syracuse University Press.

———. 1966. The Psychological Orientation of the Mother-Child Relationship in Japan. *Monumenta Nipponica* 21, no. 3–4: 322–33.

Lebra, T. 1976. *Japanese Patterns of Behavior*. Honolulu: University Press of Hawaii.

Lewis, Catherine. 1984. Cooperation and Control in Japanese Nursery Schools. *Comparative Education Review* 28 (February): 69–84.

———. 1989. From Indulgence to Internalization: Social Control in the Early School Years. *Journal of Japanese Studies* 15, no. 1 (Winter): 139–57.

Lock, Margaret. 1980. *East Asian Medicine in Urban Japan*. Berkeley and Los Angeles: University of California Press.

Monbushō (Japanese Ministry of Education, Science, and Culture). 1975. *Yōchien kyōiku yōryō* (Guidelines for Preschool Education). Tokyo: Monbushō.

———. 1981. *Preschool Education in Japan*. Tokyo: Monbushō.

———. 1985. *Statistical Abstract of Education, Science, and Culture*. Tokyo: Monbushō.

———. 1986a. *Gakkō kyōin tōkei chōsa hōkokusho* (School Faculty Statistical Survey Report). Tokyo: Monbushō.

———. 1986b. *Yōchien kyōiku no arikata ni tsuite* (The State of Preschool Education). Tokyo: Monbushō.

———. 1987. *Gakkō kihon chōsa hōkokusho* (Report on Basic Survey of Schools). Tokyo: Monbushō.

———. 1988. *Gakkō kihon chōsa hōkokusho* (Report on Basic Survey of Schools). Tokyo: Monbushō.

———. 1989. *Yōchien kyōiku Yōryō* (Guidelines for Preschool Education). Tokyo: Monbushō.

Nagano, Shigefumi. 1983. Interview, National Institute of Educational Research, Tokyo, November 24.

Norbeck, E., and M. Norbeck. 1956. Child Training in a Japanese Fishing Community. In *Personal Character and Cultural Milieu*, ed. D. Haring. Syracuse, N.Y.: Syracuse University Press.

Okada Masatoshi, Shinagawa Takako, and Moriue Shiro. 1982. *Nyūen kara sotsuen made* (From the First Day of Preschool until the Last). Asunaro Shobō, Tokyo.

Ozawa Tsunesaburo, Nishikubo Hironari, and Kusunoki Moto. 1977. *Te no kakaru kodomo no shidō* (Teaching Problem Children). Tokyo: Bunkyō Shoin.

Peak, Lois. 1986. Training Learning Skills and Attitudes in Japanese Early Educational Settings. In *Early Experience and the Development of Competence*, ed. W. Fowler. New Directions for Child Development, no. 32. San Francisco: Jossey-Bass, June.

———. 1987. "Learning to Go to School in Japan: The Transition from Home to Preschool Life." Ed.D. diss., Harvard University, Graduate School of Education.

———. 1991. Formal Pre-Elementary Education in Japan. In *Japanese Educational Productivity*, ed. Robert Leestma and H. Walberg. Ann Arbor: Center for Japanese Studies.

Rohlen, Thomas. 1989. Order in Japanese Society: Attachment, Authority, and Routine. *Journal of Japanese Studies* 15, no. 1 (Winter): 5–41.

Shigaki, Irene. 1983. Child Care Practices in Japan and the United States: How Do They Reflect Cultural Values in Young Children? *Young Children* 38 (May): 13–24.

Shinagawa Takako. 1982a. *Roku sai made ni kore dake wa* (By the Time Your Child Is Six). Tokyo: Asunaro Shobō.

———. 1982b. *San sai made ni kore dake wa* (By the Time Your Child Is Three). Tokyo: Asunaro Shobō.

Simons, Carol. 1987a. Kyoiku Mama: Secret of Japan's Schools. Condensed from *Smithsonian Magazine* in *Reader's Digest* 131 (July): 117–20.

———. 1987b. They Get By with a Lot of Help from Their Kyoiku Mamas. *Smithsonian Magazine* 17 (March): 44–53.

Statistics Bureau, Management and Coordination Agency, Japan. 1984. *Japan Statistical Yearbook 1984*. Tokyo: The Agency.

Statistics Bureau, Management and Coordination Agency, Japan. 1989. *Japan Statistical Yearbook 1989*. Tokyo: The Agency.

Stevenson, Harold. 1987. Unpublished data presented at the Conference on Social Control in Japanese Education, Green Gulch Farm Zen Center, Mill Valley, California, October.

Taniuchi (Peak), Lois. 1982. The Psychological Transition from Home to School and the Development of Japanese Children's Attitudes toward Learning. Unpublished qualifying paper, Harvard University, Graduate School of Education.

Tobin, Joseph, D. Wu, and D. Davidson. 1987. Class Size and Student/Teacher Ratios in the Japanese Preschool. *Comparative Education Review* 3, no. 4 (November): 533–49.

———. 1989. *Preschool in Three Cultures*. New Haven: Yale University Press.

Tokyo Board of Education. 1982. *Gendai oya to shite* (As a Contemporary Parent). Tokyo: Tokyo Board of Education.

United States Department of Education. *Japanese Education Today*. Washington, D.C.: U.S. Government Printing Office, 1987.

Vogel, E. 1963. *Japan's New Middle Class*. Berkeley and Los Angeles: University of California Press.

Washington Post. 1987. Summer Camp Readies Japanese Kindergartners for "Exam Hell." August 8.

White, Merry. 1987. *The Japanese Educational Challenge.* New York: Free Press.

White, Merry, and Robert LeVine. 1986. What Is an Ii Ko? In *Child Development and Education in Japan,* ed. H. Stevenson, H. Azuma, and K. Hakuta. New York: Freeman.

Yōji to hoiku (Children and Child Care). 1983. Volume 29, no. 1 (April).

Index

Academic instruction, in Japanese preschools, 77–78

Achievement, motivation for, xi–xii

Activities. *See* Routines of preschools

Adjustment problems, at home, 145–154; reluctance to attend preschool, 145–151; separation anxiety, 151–154

Adjustment problems, in the classroom, 155–183, 185; hitting, 159–165; hyperactivity, 157–159; learning to like preschool, 180–183; nonparticipation in group activities, 173–180; over-reliance on teacher, 165–173

Age, and enrollment in pre-primary schools, 195–196

aikidō (nonviolent self-defense), 179

amae (desire to be indulged), 5–6; continued longing for, 190; at home, 189; in the family, 13, 16, 185; and indulgence, 41–42; influence of the group on, 189–190; and preparation of lunch box, 93–94; and regressive dependency, 36–39; for the teacher, 165; and toilet training, 28–29, 31; and *wagamama*, 39–42

ani to issho ni iru (being together with Older Brother), 15

Arithmetic, in preschools, 65–66

asobigi (play suit), 22

Attendance at preschool, importance of, 95–96

Attendance books, 95

Authority: avoidance of overt assertion of, 186; in law and government, 188–189

Behavior, public (*soto*) vs. private (*uchi*), 189

Behavior expectations, 33–42; *amae* in family and preschool, 35–42; formal vs. informal, 185; at opening ceremony, 124; and proper roles at home and preschool, 33–35

Benkei (samurai warrior), 13

Birth rate: decline in, 195, 198; effect on preschools, 196

Boocock, Sarane, 52, 195

Box lunches (*obentō*), mothers' preparation of, 59–60

Buddhism, temple schools of, xiii–xiv

By the Time Your Child Is Three (San sai made ni kore dake wa), 54

Caudill, William, 27

Character training, as goal of preschool education, 64–65

Cheerfulness, as goal for preschoolers, 72, 73

Childrearing, and school behavior, xi

Children who need more care (*te no kakaru kodomo*), 155

Children's Garden, 102

Classmates, as teachers of group behavior, 187. *See also* Peers

Classroom routines: behavior problems in, 155–157; instructing individual children, 129, 131–132; and keeping class waiting until request accomplished, 129, 132–133; modeling correct behavior, 129–131

Clothes: changing of, 21–26, 80; description of uniforms, 21–22; for different seasons, 81; indoor and outdoor, 24; for preschoolers, 19–20; ways of managing, 24–26

Communication, mother-teacher, 123

Conflict management, 186

Davidson, D., 45, 53, 56; on box lunches, 60; on reading skills, 66; on school activities, 77; on teachers' avoidance of chastisement, 159

Text: 10/13 Palatino
Display: Palatino
Compositor: G&S Typesetters, Inc.
Printer: Braun-Brumfield, Inc.
Binder: Braun-Brumfield, Inc.